GLORY RISING

MANUAL

BOOKS BY JEFF JANSEN

Glory Rising

AVAILABLE FROM DESTINY IMAGE PUBLISHERS

GLORY RISING

KEYS TO UNDERSTANDING THE GLORY

JEFF JANSEN

Compiled by Jan Sherman

DESTINY IMAGE® PUBLISHERS, INC.

P.O. Box 310, Shippensburg, PA 17257-0310

"Speaking to the Purposes of God for This Generation and for the Generations to Come."

This book and all other Destiny Image, Revival Press, MercyPlace, Fresh Bread, Destiny Image Fiction, and Treasure House books are available at Christian bookstores and distributors worldwide.

For a U.S. bookstore nearest you, call 1-800-722-6774.

For more information on foreign distributors, call 717-532-3040.

Reach us on the Internet: www.destinyimage.com.

ISBN 10: 0-7684-3167-0

ISBN 13: 978-0-7684-3167-4

For Worldwide Distribution, Printed in the U.S.A.

1 2 3 4 5 6 7 8 9 10 11 / 13 12 11 10

Dedication

I dedicate this book to the spiritually forerunning mothers and fathers of our faith who were incredibly persecuted for demonstrating the power of the Kingdom of God in unusual miracles, signs, and wonders. These forerunning mothers and fathers willingly sacrificed all in the midst of religious misunderstanding and upheaval in order to reveal the mysteries of the secrets of our supernatural inheritance in the Kingdom of God.

I also dedicate this book to my beautiful wife, Jan, whose sacrifice, faith, and dedication has kept us on track...I love you, baby!

And I dedicate this to my children who will walk in our footsteps.

Thank You, Jesus, for Your great love and presence. We are the best of friends!

Blessings to all of you!
JEFF JANSEN

Acknowledgments

I would like to acknowledge Shae Cooke for her endless hours, hard work, and dedication in the forming of this book. Thank you for working tirelessly in the midst of so much to make this book happen. And thanks to Global Fire Ministries' staff writer and editor, Eric Green, for his contribution in helping to fill in the blanks and putting finishing touches on this project. Without you it could have taken so much longer; you were a lifesaver. A special thanks to all the intercessors and staff at Global Fire Ministries for being such a great source of strength and encouragement to Jan and myself as we tirelessly cross the globe in preaching the Gospel, trying to balance ministry and family life. We sincerely thank you.

I am deeply thankful and appreciative to my children for their understanding of ministry life and giving up of their dad. Thanks, Keenan, Hannah, James, John, Philip, and last but not least, Mercy Rain.

Thanks to Mom and Dad Jansen for consistent love. A million thank yous to Jan and Mercy Rain for your understanding hearts and selfless love in sharing me with so many. I'm looking forward to "less being more." There are so many ministry friends and family that I would like to thank personally, but to go down that road would take far too long, and I'm sure I'd leave someone out.

There are many theologians, revivalists, and wonder-workers for whom I am eternally grateful and who have forever changed my life through their ministries, writings, and testimonies of great faith. Here are but a few: William Branham, A.A. Allen, E.W. Kenyon, A.W. Tozer, Ruth Ward Heflin, Maria Woodworth-Etter, Dr. Paul Yonggi Cho, Watchman Nee, T.L. Osborn, Smith Wigglesworth, Billy Sunday, Charles Price, Kenneth Hagin, Kathryn Kuhlman, John G. Lake, Aimee Semple McPherson, John Knox, John Calvin, Charles Spurgeon, Evan Roberts, Saint Teresa of Avila, Maria of Agreda, Roland Buck, Joseph of Cupertino, Saint Anthony of Padua, Saint John Bosco, and Cornelius Jansen.

Last, I would like to thank Destiny Image for your hard work in the publishing of this work. Thanks for moving outside the realm of the accepted norm to present a supernatural gospel to the world as reality in the Kingdom of God. We love and appreciate you very much.

Endorsements

Glory Rising invites us into our role as sons and daughters of the King and heirs of the Kingdom. Through our fellowship and partnership with God, we actually release Heaven into the earth. The stories of the mystics in Church history and the present-day supernatural encounters release a hunger for what God is making available for us. The author also provides us with valuable tools for having a renewed mind and how our thanksgiving and high praise attract the Glory. This manual will challenge you to go after greater levels of supernatural experiences and a greater infilling of the Holy Spirit. The pursuit will impact and change the earth around us as His Glory is released through our alignment with Heaven.

BILL JOHNSON
Senior Pastor, Bethel Church
Redding, California
Author, *When Heaven Invades Earth* and *Face to Face with God*

Jeff Jansen is like a supernatural tour guide into the fourth dimension. His manual, *Glory Rising*, reads like a multigenerational map of the heavenly realm. Jeff invites us to join him on an amazing exploration into a fresh spiritual state of consciousness. As you experience the pages of this manual, you find yourself overcome with a new sense of God's presence. Whether you are bored in your Christian walk or you just want to reach the stars in Christ, this is for you.

KRIS VALLOTTON
Co-founder, Bethel School of Supernatural Ministry, Redding, California
Author, *The Supernatural Ways of Royalty* and
Developing a Supernatural Lifestyle

In this generation, God is raising up new voices with a fresh spirit of faith upon their lives who dare to take the Body of Christ where we have never been. One of these newly anointed vessels is my dear friend Jeff Jansen with Global Fire Ministries. It is my delight and pleasure to commend to you this contagious ministry and the writings of Jeff and Jan Jansen.

JAMES W. GOLL
Founder, Encounters Network and Prayer Storm
Author, *The Seer, Angelic Encounters, Prayer Storm,
Praying for Israel's Destiny*, and many others

Jeff is releasing a clarion call to divine encounters with the living God, calling the generations to arise and take hold of their unique destiny. In this book Jeff shares wonderful truths that will provoke you to go deeper in the Lord. Your life will be challenged as well as refreshed by the insights into the supernatural power of God. I recommend you read this book, as it will encourage your life.

BOBBY CONNER
Eagle's View Ministries

Many think they can only experience the Kingdom of Heaven when they die, but Jeff Jansen teaches you how to be normal. It is normal to experience God's Kingdom now.

SID ROTH
Host, *It's Supernatural!* television program

This book will change your perspective on Christian living forever! Jeff Jansen has beautifully articulated the Kingdom principles and supernatural ways that are available to all who hunger and thirst after righteousness. This book has the potential to challenge your spirituality to rise to the next level in God and walk in the power of the Glory generation!

JOSHUA AND JANET ANGELA MILLS
New Wine International
Palm Springs, California

I recommend this book to everyone who is hungering for Psalm 63: *"I long to see Your glory and power in the sanctuary."* I know Jeff personally and have had the joy of ministering with him many times in meetings and conferences. As Jeff ministers, a Glory river flows that releases breakthrough and power for all those who are hungry for the Lord. As Jeff shares insight and revelation on the Glory of Lord and His presence, I know you will be blessed. Get ready to come into agreement with the statement, "Fill this temple with the Glory!" We are the temple of the Holy Spirit, filled with the Glory!

KEITH MILLER
Author, *Surrender to the Spirit*
Stand Firm World Ministries

Jeff Jansen is the "real deal." I have known Jeff for several years and have directly experienced the substance of Heaven that he carries in his life. By reading this book, you will experience no less. Within this book you will not only receive fantastic, forerunning revelation about what God is doing in this hour of history, but you will also receive an impartation of the very substance of God!

Jeff Jansen is called to break the Body of Christ into something fresh and glorious, and I believe this book is loaded with enough revelation and presence of God to break you into a fresh new season of God's Glory presence in your life. Soak it up and enjoy!

RYAN WYATT
Abiding Glory Ministries

Author Jeff Jansen has done a remarkable job revealing mysteries of the Kingdom in *Glory Rising*. Jeff has had encounters with God that have resulted in every facet of his life being completely changed. His ministry is now marked by God's endorsement of signs, wonders, and miracles. By reading *Glory Rising* and by choosing to live out what the Holy Spirit has revealed in it, you too can become a supernatural carrier and demonstrator of our glorious King and His powerful Kingdom. Through walking in God's Glory, you'll become a modern day sign and wonder and part of this rising Glory generation!

JASON T. WESTERFIELD
President and founder, Kingdom Reality Ministries

Jeff Jansen's new book, *Glory Rising,* is a must-read for anyone hungering for more of the Holy Spirit in his or her life. This book will stir you to holy jealousy for the deep things of God, as well as impart a fresh passion to know the King of Glory and see His Kingdom established in the earth.

JERAME NELSON
Living at His Feet Ministries

Jeff Jansen is a true friend of God, and his writing comes from a genuine walk with the living God. This book will inspire you to reach higher, look closer, and taste and see that the Lord is good. It will challenge you to rise above the mediocrity of the masses and join the ranks of the Glory revolutionaries.

CHARLIE ROBINSON

Contents

Foreword

or many years, Bob Jones and I have prophesied the emergence of a hungry and desperate generation who would seek God wholeheartedly. Bob has called them God's "dread champions" with a heart after God like King David, who also prophesied this reality in Psalm 24 when he said:

Who may ascend into the hill of the Lord? And who may stand in His holy place? He who has clean hands and a pure heart, who has not lifted up his soul to falsehood and has not sworn deceitfully. He shall receive a blessing from the Lord and righteousness from the God of his salvation. This is the generation of those who seek Him, who seek Your face—even Jacob. Selah (Psalm 24:3-6).

This indeed is that generation of God's sons and daughters who embrace their divine destiny and overcome the spirit of this world to access Heaven and eat from the Tree of Life. A clear mandate has been placed upon this present Church Age to apprehend God's presence and Glory and reveal Him to a needy people.

The Lord will have His harvest, and God's Word will be fulfilled through a yielded and consecrated people who know the supernatural realms of Heaven and walk in its demonstration. We are now seeing the emergence of this reality, and forerunners like Jeff Jansen will introduce the winds of change into this next phase of God's perfect plan.

Through the book that you hold in your hands, Jeff has beautifully captured this prophetic perspective and provides the tools to help us access God's great grace to walk in heavenly realms and do the greater works. It will be as it was in the days of Joshua, when the Bible tells us that the Spirit that rested upon Moses was imparted to this champion to take his generation across the Jordan into the land of promise.

This book also captures biblical and historical truth, showing the convergence of the old and new as described by Jesus when He said:

Therefore every scribe who has become a disciple of the kingdom of heaven is like a head of a household, who brings out of his treasure things new and old (Matthew 13:52).

In many ways we must look back at what God has done in order to see what He is going to do. It will be as if we are going "back to the future." In the pages of this book, you will discover secrets to the anointing and walking with God by examining prior healing revivalists and champions. Jeff also teaches us how the blood of Jesus has purchased the restoration of all things going back to the personal intimacy with God and spiritual dominion lost by Adam in the Garden of Eden, as well as how we will walk in these restored realms in the 21st-century church.

Jeff also provides documented evidence of Holy Spirit exploits intended to provoke us to greater heights in God and the affirmation of our messages with signs and wonders. Clearly the early apostolic church provided a model for spiritual breakthrough and a harvest of souls. The Bible tells us how the Holy Spirit worked with the early Church fathers with the miraculous in order to confirm the message of the Kingdom. It declares in Hebrews:

After it was at the first spoken through the Lord, it was confirmed to us by those who heard, God also testifying with them, both by signs and wonders and by various miracles and by gifts of the Holy Spirit according to His own will (Hebrews 2:3-4).

Probably one of the greatest gifts Jeff has provided to us through *Glory Rising: Walking in the Realm of Creative Miracles, Signs, and Wonders* is an awakening of faith to believe for the miraculous and see God's Word demonstrated with power. Seeing the evidence of the Glory realms provokes us into desperation for more. This provides a heavenly atmosphere for miracles, signs, and wonders, fulfilling the words of Jesus when He said, *"Your Kingdom come. Your will be done on earth as it is in heaven"* (Matt. 6:10 NKJV).

Bob Jones has said, "Something has been imparted to Jeff to help mobilize today's champions to supernaturally cross over into the fullness of God's power and Glory and walk in the "mantels" demonstrated in the prior generation; the spirit of understanding is on Jeff to forerun something fresh and new."

One of the most impressive attributes Jeff has illustrated in his book is an ability to capture what have previously been considered deep, mystical realities of the Spirit and articulate them in clear, concise, and understandable ways that make them seem readily accessible. God is not looking for golden vessels or silver vessels but yielded vessels willing to devote themselves and the gifts of the Spirit to build His Kingdom—not their own. This is the clear perspective outlined in the pages of this book.

PAUL KEITH DAVIS
White Dove Ministries

BOB JONES
Bob Jones Ministries

GLORY RISING

Introduction

oward the end of his book *Prince Caspian*, C.S. Lewis has Aslan reveal Caspian's origin to him: "You come of the Lord Adam and the Lady Eve, and that is both honour enough to erect the head of the poorest beggar, and shame enough to bow the shoulders of the greatest emperor on earth."[1]

Indeed, we are the offspring of Adam and Eve—God's greatest creation, for whom He made everything. We were created as immortal beings and made in His image, and God fashioned us for a much different world, a better place than this fallen world. We don't have to wonder who we are, where we're from, or how we're to fit into this world, because God made us to fit into a perfect world. God intended us for Eden, the garden of delight.

Simply knowing that there is this perfect place helps us know that this world is a broken place, an abnormal world. Knowing that there was a time before the fall of humanity when there was perfect fellowship, communion, and harmony with God and with each other helps us understand who He intended us to be.

What great and extraordinary things could we accomplish if we lived today, in this fallen world, as we will live when supernatural Eden blooms again? God intended us for a supernatural, eternal existence; so why do we try to fit into a place never intended for us?

Though this world is fallen, it isn't worthless because it belongs to God; the earth is the Lord's and everything in it (see Ps. 24:1). He created it, and it was good, and it is worthy of restoration. Though we don't fit into it, we do fit into a supernatural life of heavenly substance in the sight of God our Creator and as active participants in the restoration of all things. As spiritual beings, we live our lives on a stage before angels and demons and the Lord of the universe in a supernatural dimension.

The Bible yields insight and perspective on what we should believe, have access to, and embrace in the divine, supernatural realm of Glory and also what we should reject as false (what satan has perverted) regarding the supernatural dimension of life.

Over the past few years especially, there have been amazing and, to some, unbelievable testimonies of tangible outward manifestations of God's Glory, such as gems, gold dust, angelic feathers, and water turning into wine, as well as third heaven encounters, angelic visitations, seer gifting, translations, and transportations.

My aim is not to promote the chasing of divine manifestations or divine supernatural encounters or experiences but to encourage Spirit-filled believers to be open and obedient to what God is doing right now and to what He wants to do in sending Glory revival through a supernatural Church.

The Bible assumes and asserts the reality of a supernatural realm, but our modernistic society has ingrained within us a skeptical mind-set that it's not real, it's illegitimate, or it's not for us today. Consequently, mainstream Christianity tends to dismiss the authentic supernatural things of God (supernatural experiences, power, ability, encounters, and outward or tangible manifestations of His Glory) to evangelistic endeavors or to the biblical eras of the apostles, Enoch, Elijah, Gehazi, and others. In a way, we've played down and even suppressed its activity, perhaps in fear or misapprehension of breaching "legal" spiritual boundaries. People pray to a supernatural God, but when He does supernatural things, they attribute it to the devil.

Yet almost one-third of the Scriptures involve dreams, visions, and God communing with His people. A growing number of Christians today are experiencing God in this way—speaking, seeing, feeling, and even doing things with Him in the spiritual realm. These acts and experiences of intimate communion will spur the next great Glory revival, for God says, in the last days:

> *…I will pour forth of My Spirit on all mankind; and your sons and your daughters shall prophesy, and your young men shall see visions, and your old men shall dream dreams* (Acts 2:17).

For the most part, we've had a theologically informed worldview that has seamlessly matched reality. But God has called us to that place of heavenly perspective, the Glory realm, and the reality of the supernatural in our daily lives. It's a radical shift from an earthly perspective to a heavenly one.

As God's children, *imago deo,* made in His image and likeness as spiritual beings, we have similar faculties of mind, will, and emotion to the Father. Like begets like, so in truth, each one of us has the potential to walk, live, and have our being in the supernatural ways of God in order to fulfill our mission and very purpose for being here.

Those who sow in tears shall reap in joy. He who continually goes forth weeping, bearing seed for sowing, shall doubtless come again with rejoicing, bringing his sheaves with him (Psalm 126:5-6 NKJV).

It all started in a garden where God placed His newly created son, and it was in that garden where he fell from the Glory of God. So it was in another garden, far removed from Eden, where Christ wept with great tears and agony that would restore humankind to the original place from which we fell—from the Glory! However, He wept for the joy that was set before Him, interceding for us, sowing in tears, knowing that His weeping would bring forth great seed of Kingdom harvest. For the joy that was set before Him, He endured the Cross (see Heb. 12:2). The joy set before Him is us.

We are at a time, right now, when God is reaping the very thing Jesus sowed in seed form in the Garden—His offspring, who are doing the very works of the Kingdom of God. Jesus shed His blood for this very reason, and the Father is overjoyed in seeing His children bringing back sheaves of harvest and generating fruit born out of His suffering.

It is the Father's good pleasure to give us the Kingdom. The return of the Glory of the Lord is at hand, and it's time for us to step into high places and into our inheritance, which we can begin living in now.

Endnote

1.   C.S. Lewis, *Prince Caspian: The Return to Narnia* (New York: Collier Books, 1951), 211-212.

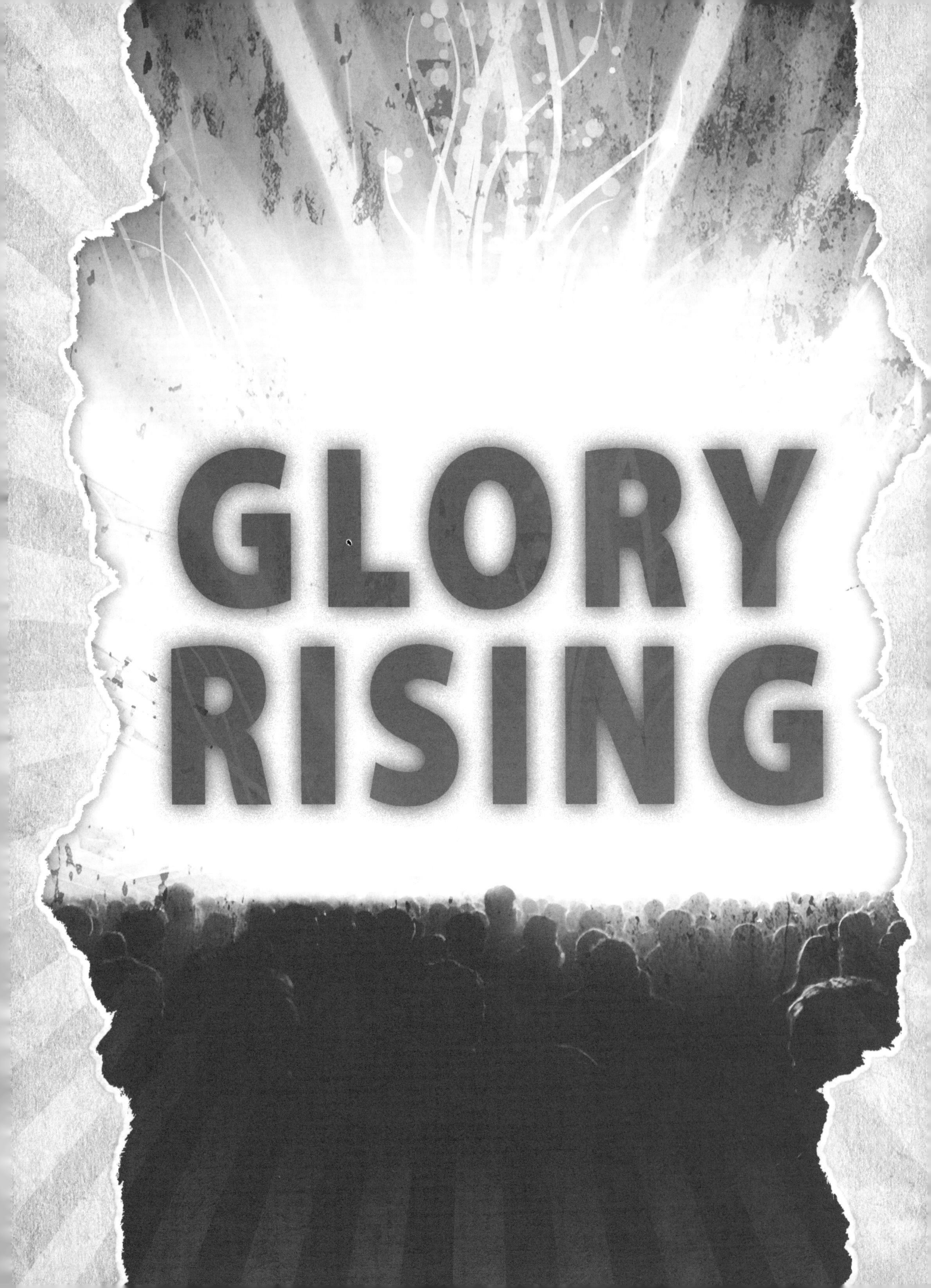
GLORY
RISING

Chapter 1

ACCESS TO EDEN

s Spirit-filled believers with our roots in Eden, we should live our lives as we will live eternity. Creator God, at great cost, has opened the way back to Eden, which, for every believer, should be a true view of supernatural reality.

The atoning sacrifice of Jesus provided not only for the salvation of humanity, but also for the restoration and reconciliation of the whole creation, even *exceeding* the glories of the original creation (see Col. 1:20).

God's desire is to have a people who will rightly display and secure His Glory and the power of the Kingdom of God throughout the world. Indeed, this is what we were created for—to secure the Glory of God in Heaven.

Our occupation as God's spiritual children is to carry the Kingdom of God everywhere we go. Jesus displayed this as the first of a new breed of Man. He was a Spirit-filled Son of God who role-modeled what we were to do as Spirit-filled sons and daughters of the Kingdom.

We were created…to secure the Glory of God in Heaven.

The Lord is looking for His Church to keep its head focused in the heavens above and its body fixed on the earth below, walking out the Kingdom mandate with all-convincing demonstrations of

His power. To do this, we must reconnect with the Head (Jesus Christ), the *last Adam,* and grow up spiritually (see Eph. 4:15).

Questions to Ponder

What was the "great cost" God paid to open the way back to Eden? How does coming back to Eden affect our view of spiritual reality?

_____

_____

_____

_____

What is the focus of the Church? How do you think we are to maintain relevancy in both the Kingdom of Heaven and the Kingdom on earth?

_____

_____

_____

_____

The Concept of the Kingdom

The concept of a Kingdom *originated* in the mind of God and *began* in the Garden of Eden. It was in the heart of God to have a royal family of sons and daughters, a community of humanity who would love Him and daily walk with Him in relationship, extending the blessings of that close communion with Elohim to all of creation. Humans were to fill the earth, subdue it, and rule over it, sharing God's rule and reign in kingly authority (see Gen. 1:26).

The essence of a Kingdom is property. Humankind cannot govern something that isn't there. Property or land validates and defines a king or ruler and gives one the right to claim kingship or rulership. Thus, God created the Kingdom territory or colony called "earth" and then He created humans to be *His legal representatives* over this physical Kingdom territory, giving them dominion over the earth (see Ps. 8:6).

> *Then God said, "Let Us make man in Our image, according to Our likeness; and let them rule over the fish of the sea and over the birds of the sky and over the cattle and over all the earth, and over every creeping thing that creeps on the earth" (Genesis 1:26).*

Questions to Ponder

What is the concept of the Kingdom? What is its essence?

_____

_____

_____

_____

_____

Adam, the Firstborn Son of God

God the Father raised Adam from the ground by His supernatural breath. When the Father breathed into Adam's nostrils the breath of life, the DNA of the Creator was deposited into his spirit, soul, and body. Adam, with the Spirit of God in him, was created a supernatural being with the ability to create and co-create with God by the power of the Spirit.

Adam, as the firstborn son of God, was completely natural and supernatural. Above all of his capabilities, his most valuable and precious one was that of knowing, loving, and obeying his Creator. He knew God, and his love for God was pure, his obedience to God unfailing, and thus, his joy and happiness freely and naturally flowed.

*When the Father breathed into Adam's nostrils the breath of life, the
DNA of the Creator was deposited into his spirit, soul, and body.*

For a while, Adam was incapable of suffering; he was immortal and nothing could taint his joy. He was God's offspring, a son of His love, fruit of His own nature, created in His image. He was an authoritative son and functioned *in the full power* of this government of the earth as co-ruler, prince, and governor.

God gave to Adam perfect powers and capacities, inherent power and ability. His faculties were supernatural, and therein Adam was more than capable and qualified to govern over every living thing that moved upon the earth—over everything that God had made by the works of His hands. Adam was the conduit between God and creation.

Adam's naming of the animals called for a high level of revelation and discernment because the fate and future of every living creature resided in Adam. The name of each animal would define the species' very nature. Whatever Adam said they were was the nature they assumed. As His offspring, God called Adam to call those things that were not as though they were (see Rom. 4:17).

*(as it is written, "I have made you a father of many nations") in the presence
of Him whom he believed—God, who gives life to the dead and calls those
things which do not exist as though they did (Romans 4:17 NKJV).*

When Adam rebelled against God, however, he abdicated his governorship-regency, essentially passing it to the devil by default because the devil had no rightful claim or authority to take it. Adam's refusal to comply with God's instructions regarding the two trees actually *deprived* his human mind of access to godly knowledge and spiritual things and confined it to the pursuit of physical knowledge. Humankind has gained and applied much physical knowledge since the days of Adam. However, government involves the *application* of spiritual principles to be genuinely successful by those governing or ruling, and likewise, by those being ruled.[1]

Questions to Ponder

What were some of the characteristics of the firstborn son of God, Adam? What kind of relationship did he have with creation? What was his relationship with God like? What special abilities did he have?

_____

_____

_____

_____

What is the difference between godly knowledge and physical knowledge? In which knowledge have you developed the most? How are we to learn and increase in godly knowledge?

_____

_____

_____

_____

The Last Adam

What Adam lost in the Garden, Jesus Christ reopened and regained, and He has given it back to humankind. Jesus became Adam again to successfully inject the full DNA of God's original intent back into the earth and our lives so that *we* can now walk in it. Jesus took dominion over the earth, called those things that were not as though they were, and multiplied His disciples. And the disciples later turned the world upside down. Jesus communed with the Father regularly, performed creative and re-creative miracles, effected signs and wonders, subdued His enemies, and in His final awesome and great act of dominion and ruling on earth, conquered death. This immortality is a testimony to us of what the first Adam's life was to be in that ancient garden and what ours is to be now—a perfect, supernatural existence in relationship with God the Father, the Creator of the universe.

Thus it is written, the first man Adam became a living being (an individual personality); the last Adam (Christ) became a life-giving Spirit [restoring the dead to life] (1 Corinthians 15:45 AMP).

Questions to Ponder

Why did Jesus become Adam again? What opportunities did this open up for the original disciples and us today?

_____

_____

_____

_____

_____

_____

Reconnected to Eden

And God purposed that through Him all things should be completely reconciled back to Him (see Col. 1:20). What does God want reconciled back to Him? All things. What are "all things"? Everything that was lost in Eden—Kingdom authority, sonship, and the ability to move in the ways of God.

Adam was clothed in light. The Glory of God *clothed* Adam. God wants to walk with us in the ways of Eden as He did with Adam in the cool of the day—He wants us to be clothed in His Glory. Adam was an incredible creation. He was a co-creator with God. Everything God created in the heavens and the earth He did with words.

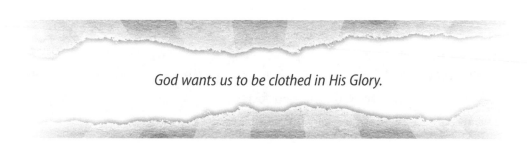

God wants us to be clothed in His Glory.

God wants us to speak like this again, creating and recreating the world around us in Glory. Jesus Christ opened up for us the way, which was sealed off in the Garden: the Tree of Life—access to Eden. The Father opened up a new and living way for us again through Jesus Christ. This was the original position He created Adam to walk in—access into the presence of God.

Questions to Ponder

In what ways are we to be reconnected to Eden? How are we to walk in the reconciliation we have obtained through Christ?

_____

_____

_____

_____

_____

_____

Endnote

1. Brian Orchard, "Power to the People," *Vision,* http://www.vision.org/visionmedia/article.aspx?id=137 (accessed December 13, 2008).

QUESTIONS FOR GROUP DISCUSSION

"The Lord is looking for His Church to keep its head focused in the heavens above and its body fixed on the earth below." What does that mean in the practical sense for us as we live our daily lives?

_____

_____

_____

_____

_____

_____

_____

_____

_____

_____

Explain and discuss the meaning of First Corinthians 15:45 (AMP): *"Thus it is written, the first man Adam became a living being (an individual personality); the last Adam (Christ) became a life-giving Spirit (restoring the dead to life)."*

_____

_____

_____

_____

_____

_____

_____

_____

LIFE APPLICATION

If "God's desire is to have a people who will rightly display and secure His Glory and the power of the Kingdom of God throughout the world," how does this affect your job description for the rest of your life? How does this affect your priorities? What changes do you need to make in your life?

_____

_____

_____

_____

_____

_____

_____

_____

_____

_____

_____

_____

_____

_____

_____

_____

_____

_____

_____

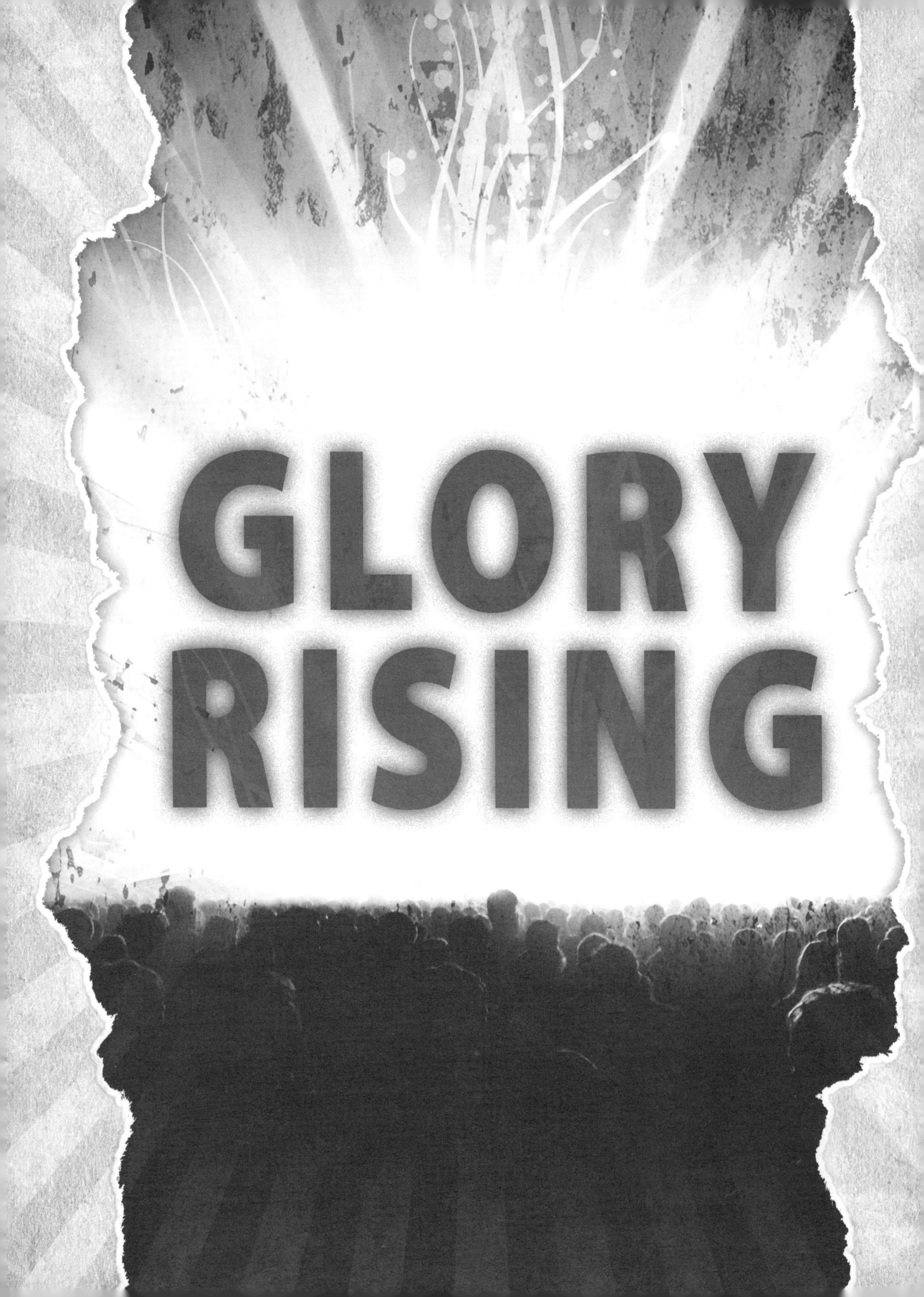
GLORY
RISING

Chapter 2

THE KINGDOM MANDATE

The Kingdom of Heaven is advancing on the earth at an incredible rate. We are beginning to witness the coming forth of past seeds sown into humanity—both good and evil. The intercessory prayers made by the saints over the last two millennia will release a shockwave of the Glory of God in the earth never witnessed in the history of humankind. As this happens, we will see a massive Kingdom shift that will result in the harvest coming with alarming demonstrations of supernatural signs, wonders, miracles, healing, and deliverance. The Body of Christ is coming into a unity in the Spirit that will grow into a maturity in the full knowledge of Jesus, arriving at the complete and total measure and stature of the fullness in Christ (see Eph. 4:13). In order for this to happen, we must know the power of the Gospel we preach and what our mandate is.

Questions to Ponder

What are the marks that show the "Body of Christ is coming into a unity of the Spirit"? Do you see any of these marks on the Christians around you?

_____

_____

_____

_____

_____

What do you think are the signs that will let us know that we have grown into the "full knowledge of Jesus"? How do you personally seek to mature in Christ?

_____

_____

_____

_____

_____

_____

What Gospel?

Jesus did not come preaching salvation, nor did He preach miracles, deliverance, or healing. Jesus came preaching the gospel of the Kingdom; and as He did, He manifested deliverance, healing, signs, and wonders. The majority of His parables were about the Kingdom of God. Jesus mentions or talks about the Kingdom of Heaven or the Kingdom of God 129 times in the four Gospels alone, making it His most talked about subject.

When the Kingdom is preached, there should *always* be a demonstration of power—whether it's manifested as a physical healing or miracle, or a spiritual rebirth causing a transformation of the mind and heart. Signs, wonders, miracles, healings, and other outflowings of power *always* follow the preaching of the *genuine* gospel of the Kingdom.

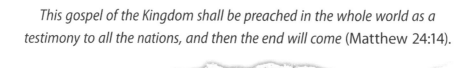

This gospel of the Kingdom shall be preached in the whole world as a testimony to all the nations, and then the end will come (Matthew 24:14).

For the kingdom of God does not exist in words but in power (1 Corinthians 4:20).

[Even as my preaching has been accompanied] with the power of signs and wonders, [and all of it] by the power of the Holy Spirit. [The result is] that starting from Jerusalem and

as far round as Illyricum, I have fully preached the Gospel [faithfully executing, accomplishing, carrying out to the full the good news] of Christ (the Messiah) in its entirety (Romans 15:19 AMP).

For I am not ashamed of the gospel, for it is the power of God for salvation to everyone who believes… (Romans 1:16).

Questions to Ponder

Did you know that Jesus did not preach salvation? What significance does the Kingdom of God have to humanity?

_____

_____

_____

_____

_____

_____

Why do "signs, wonders, miracles, healings, and other outflowings of power *always* follow the preaching of the *genuine* gospel of the Kingdom"? Is there a conclusion to be made as to why we are not seeing the signs and wonders today that the early church experienced?

_____

_____

_____

_____

_____

_____

Kingdom Dominion

Your Kingdom come Your will be done, on earth as it is in heaven (Matthew 6:10).

From time to time I'll hear someone say, "If I only knew the will of God for my life…." From the verse in Matthew, Jesus makes it very clear how to know His perfect will; we can conclude that God's will is *His Kingdom being birthed on the earth.*

God's intent is that His will be done on earth just like it is being done in Heaven—that the physical domain of earth would resemble the spiritual domain of Heaven, as an extension or a territory of the Kingdom of God in Heaven. His original plan was to extend His heavenly domain on the earth through a family of sons and daughters—not servants.

Servants have no authority and are not part of the Father's house, but serve as subjects in the master's quarters (see Galatians 4:1-7).

The Father's plan was that as his sons and daughters, we would share His rulership as a family of sons and daughters who would rule the earth on His behalf.

Questions to Ponder

According to Matthew 6:10, what is God's will for your life? What does this mean on a day-to-day basis for your life?

_____

_____

_____

_____

_____

_____

Subdue the Earth

The first commandment God gave humankind was to subdue the earth and have dominion (see Gen. 1:26-30). This command was hindered when Adam fell and surrendered the earth to satan. Through Jesus' death and resurrection, He took back the keys of the Kingdom, the authority and rightful dominion of earth, and gave them back to humankind. Furthermore, born-again children of God have the privilege and capacity to co-labor with Christ to establish and advance His Kingdom on the earth.

We are citizens of a heavenly Kingdom, a Kingdom not of this world (see Phil. 3:20; John 18:36). Because we are citizens of Heaven, we have a legal right to access all the blessings of Heaven. We know that there is no sickness in Heaven, no disease, no poverty, no depression, no sin, and no broken families. Therefore, we have authorized permission to take those things and *manifest them on earth.*

We are the offspring of God; we have our Father's royal blood and DNA flowing through our spirits.

Jesus is the King of many kings and Lord of many lords (see Rev. 19:16; 1 Tim. 6:15). We are the kings and lords over earth. Heaven is God's territory, and earth is humanity's territory. God designed us for the rule of earth, not the rule of Heaven.

Questions to Ponder

What do the words of your job description—to "subdue" and have "dominion"—mean to you?

_____

_____

_____

_____

_____

Do you believe you have the capacity inside of you to be a king and lord over planet Earth? Why or why not?

_____

_____

_____

_____

_____

_____

Spiritual Aerodynamics

Jesus proclaimed the same words as John the Baptist, *"Repent, for the Kingdom of Heaven is at hand"* (Matt. 4:17). That message was not only for individuals in and through whom the Kingdom was to be established, but also for the Church. It was a call to turn from our old way of thinking and embrace Kingdom thinking because the Kingdom of God is *now*.

The act of repentance is changing our way of thinking from the natural to the spiritual. It is discarding, turning from, and abandoning former thought patterns and processes and adopting the Source of all truth—Jesus Christ. True repentance is receiving the mind of Christ and aligning ourselves (spirit, soul, and body) with the Kingdom of Heaven.

Jesus told Nicodemus (see John 3:1-8) that in order to *see* the Kingdom of God in operation, he must be born from above. He was saying to Nicodemus that he could never see the Kingdom, nor experience it, unless he was first born from another dimension—a higher dimension. We could also say that we must be "borne" or lifted from above. We must be airborne—lifted from the natural ways of thinking and understanding—into a higher reality.

Therefore if you have been raised up with Christ, keep seeking the things above, where Christ is, seated at the right hand of God. Set your mind on the things above, not on the things that are on earth (Colossians 3:1-2).

Gaining God's perspective is one of the keys that will bring about the last-day harvest. When we see the world around us with the eyes of Christ, we have tapped into the realm of *all things are possible.*

The Kingdom mind-set is superior to the natural mind-set. Those born of the flesh are born from the natural realm and are *subject to natural laws.* However, those born of the Spirit are spirit and are *no longer* subject to the natural.

The essence of repentance has very little to do with feeling sorry for something bad we've done, but rather turning from our old earthly way of thinking to a new heavenly way of being.

Questions to Ponder

Describe the difference between a heavenly, Kingdom mind-set and an earthly, natural mind-set. How do you see yourself in terms of where your mind-set is?

_____

_____

_____

_____

_____

_____

Define "repentance" in your own words. How does repentance relate to seeing Kingdom possibilities for your life?

_____

_____

_____

_____

_____

_____

The Family Business

It's high time for us now to be about the Father's business. Jesus is the firstborn among many brothers (see Rom. 8:29). The only begotten Son is the prototype for the brothers and sisters who, with Him, become the heirs of the coming Kingdom.

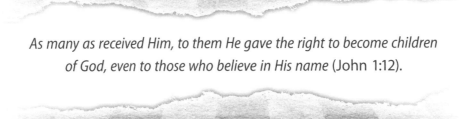

As many as received Him, to them He gave the right to become children of God, even to those who believe in His name (John 1:12).

We are starting to see the children of the Kingdom come into maturity. Through His offspring, God is manifesting and establishing His Kingdom and His will on earth.

Everywhere that He preached the gospel, Jesus manifested His power with wild miracles, signs, and wonders. God expects His offspring, His family, His seed to do the same works—acting the same way as Jesus did. All things have been put in subjection under the feet of Christ. We are the Body of Christ—so all things have been put under our feet.

Questions to Ponder

What does knowing that Jesus is your Firstborn Brother do for your confidence in doing Kingdom work?

_____

_____

_____

_____

_____

_____

_____

What standard has He set for you?

_____

_____

_____

_____

_____

_____

_____

_____

_____

QUESTIONS FOR GROUP DISCUSSION

If you were to describe the "Kingdom mandate" to someone else, how would you explain this concept? What details are necessary to fully participate in this mandate?

_____

_____

_____

_____

_____

_____

_____

_____

_____

_____

In your opinion, what does it mean to "act the same way as Jesus did"? What are the components of His lifestyle?

_____

_____

_____

_____

_____

_____

_____

_____

_____

_____

LIFE APPLICATION

What has this section taught you about the true nature of repentance and what it opens up to you as a believer? How will you enlist the Holy Spirit to realign repentance in your daily prayer life so you can gain a heavenly perspective? In what ways do you feel called to advance the Kingdom of God in the earth? What has the Lord spoken to you about your involvement and destiny concerning the *Kingdom Mandate*?

_____

_____

_____

_____

_____

_____

_____

_____

_____

_____

_____

_____

_____

_____

_____

_____

_____

GLORY RISING

Chapter 3

CATCHING A GLIMPSE
OF ETERNITY

…He has also set eternity in the hearts of men… (Ecclesiastes 3:11 NIV).

hroughout the ages there have been many mystical wonder-workers who performed incredible signs throughout the world. These revivalists and mystical wonder-workers moved in raw supernatural power that flowed from an intimate union with Christ.

God is still sending ecstatic mystical wonder-workers today to shake and wake the Body of Christ from the status quo into the reality of the realm of Glory. Starting with Jesus and looking throughout Church history, we find that these stories of God's mighty hand cause a fresh passion, faith, and expectancy for us to seize the promises of God in our own lives, and launch us further into His unfolding plan.

Questions to Ponder

Have you had questions about the veracity of the testimonies of mystics and stories of their experiences? What do you think you need to do to come into a true understanding of the nature of these accounts?

_____

_____

_____

_____

Do you think it's possible for these same experiences to happen today? To you? Why or why not?

_____

_____

_____

_____

_____

Jesus, the "Mystic Secret of God"

During His life on earth, Jesus flawlessly modeled to us a natural man in right relationship with a supernatural God. He was still fully God but emptied Himself into a body of flesh, becoming fully man. Jesus was *"...made like His brethren in all things"* (Heb. 2:17).

One of the reasons He was "made like His brethren in *all* things" was to give us an example of what a human being could access, accomplish, and overcome by the Spirit, grace, and power of God. Before Jesus was baptized in the Holy Spirit, there were no accounts of miracles, healings, or casting out of demons. He was a Man—a simple carpenter who sought to please His Father in Heaven.

It was after being baptized with the Holy Spirit that signs, wonders, and miracles flooded His ministry. We know that we have access to everything Jesus walked in because He was a man in right relationship with God. He even said that we would do greater works than Him (see John 14:12).

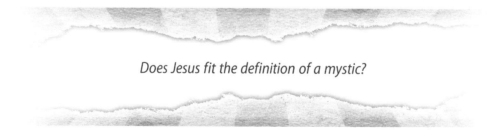

Does Jesus fit the definition of a mystic?

Webster's New World Dictionary defines a *mystic* as "one who professes to undergo profound spiritual experiences." It defines *mysticism* as "belief in the possibility of attaining direct communion with God or knowledge of spiritual truths, as by meditation." Does Jesus fit this definition of a mystic? I don't think Jesus fits the definition of a mystic—I think He *created* the definition!

For too long the occult has claimed words like *mystic, meditation, experience,* and *new age.* Poor Christian doctrine states that godly supernatural experiences stopped after the first century. In reality, without the supernatural we wouldn't be here. The universe wouldn't exist; the family of Israel wouldn't have been delivered out of Egypt; Jesus would never have come in the flesh or risen from the dead. Without the supernatural, the early Church would have taken a nosedive—3,000 people would not have been saved that first day.

The recent New Age movement has revealed the heart cry of a generation to truly understand and participate in the supernatural realm. It shows us that mainstream Christianity hasn't stewarded properly the supernatural endowments of God. It's time for the Church to arise with a genuine demonstration of power.

The New Age movement is primarily distinguished by a desire for spiritual exploration. A large sect of New Agers believes in oneness with nature. Jesus spoke to creation on numerous occasions—not only existing in unison with creation, but exercising dominion over it too. Jesus existed in harmony with creation even on a subatomic level—defying what some would call "natural laws." He flew (see Acts 1:9). He walked on water as a man (see Matt. 14:24-26). He walked through walls (see John 20:26). When we come into agreement with Jesus Christ, harmonizing wholly with the Word of God, we can actually, like Jesus, defy natural laws and display supernatural ability.

Questions to Ponder

> Does Jesus fit the definition of a mystic as described in *Webster's New World Dictionary*? How would you describe Jesus' mysticism to someone else?

_____

_____

_____

_____

_____

> What does the New Age movement reveal about the yearning of people's souls and spirits? What does the Church need to do in order to satisfy the cry for spiritual exploration of this generation?

_____

_____

_____

_____

_____

_____

Intimacy and Ecstasy

God is calling us to a place of intimate ecstasy. We are designed to experience God with all of our senses, both spiritual and natural. We are called to dwell in the eternal ecstasy of God's presence and love—personally and experientially.

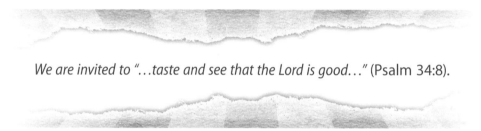

We are invited to "…taste and see that the Lord is good…" (Psalm 34:8).

The past is filled with mystical wonder-workers who intimately encountered God in supernatural ways. These men and women were caught into trancelike visions, raptures, and ecstasies of God's love. They would physically levitate off the ground and even fly. They were taken to Heaven, encountered angels, and were transported, translated, and bilocated!

St. Teresa of Avila

One of these is **St. Teresa of Avila** (1515-1582), one of the many Catholic saints known for extreme ecstatic spiritual encounters. St. Teresa of Avila penned several great works, including *Interior Castle.* In this writing, she talks about the process of four levels or degrees of communion with God. The first is the incomplete mystic union that comes with the quieting of the mind—simple contemplation. The second is the full or semi-ecstatic union with God she sometimes referred to as the "prayer of union." The third level she describes as ecstatic union, or complete ecstasy. The fourth level she depicts is absolute oneness with God—a spiritual marriage between God and the soul.

When we go deep into ecstasy, it turns into a trancelike experience. In Acts 10:10, Peter fell into a trance. It was a type of ecstasy where the natural world around him was blurred, which allowed him to clearly see and hear in the Spirit at a heightened sense. The deepest level of an ecstatic trance is where we become so unaware of our natural surroundings and so clearly focused on the eternal realm that we're not really sure whether we are on earth, in Heaven, or even in or out of our bodies, just as Paul did in Second Corinthians 12:1-4.

Trances were common in the life and ministry of **Maria Woodworth-Etter** (1844-1924), a traveling preacher during the Holiness and Pentecostal Movements. Some would consider her the grandmother of the Pentecostal movement because she embraced speaking in tongues, trances, visions, dancing, singing, and other outward manifestations of God's presence, including being *slain in the Spirit,* a term that likely originated from her meetings.

Maria Woodworth-Etter

Question to Ponder

Why do you think God speaks so clearly and provides incredible experiences to people during trances?

_____

_____

_____

_____

_____

Supernatural Downloads

A trance is a means of being open to hear God's voice and receive revelation from the supernatural realm of Heaven. In this place of ecstasy, our spiritual senses are heightened and our unrenewed minds come into submission and obedience to the things of the Spirit. We receive supernatural downloads of heavenly knowledge, revelation, and wisdom. We become open to receive the counsel of the Spirit (see 1 Cor. 2:10,12-14).

One man who received extreme supernatural downloads of revelation was **St. Ignatius** (1491-1556), founder of the Jesuit Order. Once, while recovering from severe sickness, he was lifted off the ground in prayer in the kneeling position. Onlookers heard his prayer: "O, my God, how can I love You as You deserve. If men but knew You, they would never offend You; for they would love You too much to do so."[1]

St. Ignatius

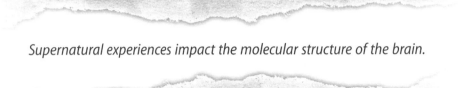

Supernatural experiences impact the molecular structure of the brain.

Roland Buck with his dog Queenie

Another man who received downloads of supernatural revelation was **Roland Buck** (1918-1979), an Assembly of God pastor in Boise, Idaho. During a season of encounters, he was sucked up to the throne room where he received supernatural knowledge about the Bible and the nature of God. Burned into his mind were 2,000 Scripture passages that he could quote at any time. When talking to him, people said it was like talking to a Bible; his words and ideas were bathed in Scripture.

Supernatural downloads of knowledge are not uncommon in the Body of Christ today. Supernatural experiences impact the molecular structure of the brain, causing it to receive information much like a computer receives an upgrade. More frequently, people's minds are being renewed and transformed by these powerful mystical ecstatic experiences.

In the coming days, we will witness an increase in supernatural revelation that will also greatly benefit the sciences. There will be new inventions, alternate energy sources, and the capability of restructuring the molecular makeup all the way down to a single atom. Even now angels are visiting believers, giving them formulas and blueprints to help bring these things about. The unthinkable will be thinkable—the undoable will be done!

Questions to Ponder

What effect does a trance have on our senses and their ability to be receptors of God's revelation, wisdom, and knowledge?

_____

_____

_____

_____

_____

_____

Have you ever experienced a supernatural download from Heaven? Why is this an appropriate way for God to change the course of a life or world history?

_____

_____

_____

_____

_____

Endnote

1. Mary Purcell, *The First Jesuit, St. Ignatius Loyola* (Chicago: Loyola University Press, 1981), 71.

QUESTIONS FOR GROUP DISCUSSION

Have you read any writings of the mystics from history? What impact might the revelations from these people do to stir your faith and openness to the supernatural?

_____

_____

_____

_____

_____

_____

_____

_____

_____

Explore your feelings about biblically based spiritual trances. What excites you about the possibility of experiencing these ecstatic events? What are your misgivings?

_____

_____

_____

_____

_____

_____

_____

_____

LIFE APPLICATION

Throughout this chapter we have seen people who were in love with God to such an extent that they experienced God's power, love, and abilities in supernatural ways. Are you tending your love of God so that you may be in a position to receive the same types of experiences in your life? How might you increase your love?

_____

_____

_____

_____

_____

_____

_____

_____

_____

_____

_____

_____

_____

_____

GLORY RISING

Chapter 4

MYSTICAL WONDER-WORKERS PAST AND PRESENT

When supernatural signs, wonders, and miracles are performed, they impart to the viewer a fresh vigor to cast off the detrimental restraints of doubt, fear, and unbelief. They act as a catalyst to propel them into deeper realms of faith, trust, and reliance in Jesus Christ.

It is the Spirit of God who gives us the ability to move and operate in Kingdom principles and realities (see 1 Cor. 12:9-10). In this hour, God is pouring out fresh waves of His Spirit, and He expects us to move in supernatural phenomena that give Him Glory.

To you it has been given to know the secrets and mysteries of the kingdom of heaven... (Matthew 13:11 AMP).

An impartation of wonder-working faith is ready to be manifested in your own life. These mantels are yours for the taking! Surrender old paradigms to the Holy Spirit and let Him be your guide in the supernatural Kingdom of Heaven—you'll never be the same!

Questions to Ponder

What do seeing signs, wonders, and miracles do to you as a believer?

_____

_____

_____

_____

_____

_____

Do these experiences challenge your faith or help increase it?

_____

_____

_____

_____

_____

_____

Translation of the Spirit

Translation is a unique experience where the spirit of a person is lifted from his or her body and is brought to another place by the Spirit of God or sometimes by angels. Being translated in the Holy Spirit is one of the many ways God can speak and reveal the mysteries of His Kingdom to us. Two people in the Bible who experienced translation were Elisha and Paul (see 2 Kings 5:26; Col. 2:5; 1 Cor. 5:3).

For even though I am absent in body, nevertheless I am with you in spirit, rejoicing to see your good discipline and the stability of your faith in Christ (Colossians 2:5).

Translation experiences are more than visionary encounters; the spirit of a person is actually present in a different location. During these experiences, the person has the ability to see and hear the events taking place and gain detailed knowledge of specific circumstances.

Question to Ponder

Read the Scriptures listed: Second Kings 5:26; Colossians 2:5; and First Corinthians 5:3: What do you see in these Scriptures that allows you to understand how your spirit can be translated from one place to another?

_____

_____

_____

_____

Transportation of the Body

Transportation is when the spirit, soul, and body of a person are transported to another location. Unlike translation, where only the spirit of a person travels, transportation is when the entire person is physically transported to a different location. Transportation occurs when a portal opens in the spirit and a person goes through it. The Holy Spirit Himself is a type of portal who can take us places (see Acts 8:39-40; 2 Kings 2:11; Rev. 4:1-2).

Question to Ponder

Read the Scriptures listed: Acts 8:39-40; Second Kings 2:11; and Revelation 4:1-2: What do you see in these Scriptures that allows you to understand how your body can be transported from one place to another?

_____

_____

_____

_____

The Wonderful Gift of Bilocation

Bilocation occurs when a person is present in two places simultaneously. Although there are no instances of this unique manifestation recorded in the Bible, there are numerous documented accounts of bilocation in the lives of saints. Bilocation can be categorized with translation and transportation. However, instead of the saint's spirit traveling to a different location, or his entire spirit, soul, and body doing so, bilocation occurs when he is tangibly in two locations at the same time.

Unlike the natural realm, there is no distance or time in the realm of the spirit.

St. Alphonsus Liguori

St. Alphonsus Liguori (1696-1787) was seen by credible witnesses to be in two different locations at the same time on several occasions. One of the most astonishing reports is during the death of Pope Clement XIV. The saint fell into a trance for nearly two days without showing any sign of life. During the experience, he was assisting the Pope during his death. Not long afterward, everyone received the news that Pope Clement XIV had passed away around 7:00 A.M. on September 22. This was the same time St. Alphonsus came out of the trance.

St. Joseph of Cupertino

St. Joseph of Cupertino (1603-1663) bilocated to assist an elderly friend. The elderly gentleman asked St. Joseph if he would assist him at the hour of his death. The saint agreed and added, "I shall assist you, even though I should be in Rome." Indeed, while St. Joseph was in Rome, his friend became sick. During the last hour of his life, those caring for him saw St. Joseph speaking with him.[1]

Venerable Maria of Agreda
"Lady in Blue"

Ven. Maria of Agreda (1602-1665), a nun, not only bilocated across Spain and Portugal, but also crossed the Atlantic to visit America. In 1620, while immersed in ecstatic prayer, Maria was transported to New Mexico, where she was commanded by the Lord Jesus to teach the Indians. Later, when questioned, she could accurately describe the province in New Mexico. Over the next 11 years, Maria bilocated over 500 times.

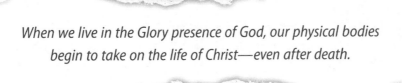

*When we live in the Glory presence of God, our physical bodies
begin to take on the life of Christ—even after death.*

Additionally, Maria's physical body refuses to let the process of decay take over. After more than 320 years, her body is still pristine and unsusceptible to decay.[2] When we live in the Glory presence of God, our physical bodies begin to take on the life of Christ—even after death. This is another mystical sign that causes us to stop and wonder.

Question to Ponder

Read the accounts of the saints listed: St. Alphonsus Liguori; St. Joseph of Cupertino; and Ven. Maria of Agreda. What do you see in these accounts that allows you to understand how we can bilocate from one place to another? (I encourage you to research for yourself the lives of these saints to gain a deeper understanding of the supernatural and also to see that they were very much human, no different from me or you.)

_____

_____

_____

_____

_____

The Visitation

I remember after prayer one night, I was pulled out of my body, through the roof, through the atmosphere, and past the stars, and I came to rest in a large room in Heaven called the Room of Intercession. I saw men, women, children, and angels all praying over the nations. I saw the regions of the earth flash before me in a moment of time. As I was watching, praise began to flow from my spirit man.

Glory Cloud

As I awoke, my eyes were opened to a whole new dimension in the Spirit. Rainbows would appear in meetings, clouds of Glory would manifest, and miracles would explode in the atmosphere with tangible signs of the Glory. God had changed the ministry and our lives, and we would never be the same.

God had changed the ministry...and we would never be the same.

One significant event happened at a meeting in Cincinnati, Ohio. The conference, with 1,200 participants, started on a Thursday night. I told the host pastors that I would not be there Thursday because of a pre-arranged event but would drive to Cincinnati early Friday morning. I did exactly that. I kept my appointment in Nashville where, during our communion time, my body became electric with the fire of God. I felt like I was expanding and would come apart. This experience happened for what seemed like an hour.

Question to Ponder

What are the experiences of your life that demonstrate the power of God to go beyond what you think is possible?

_____

_____

_____

_____

_____

_____

_____

_____

_____

The Heavenly Visitor

I drove all night and arrived in Cincinnati at 8:30 A.M. Friday. I sat down with the other speakers and was in the sessions all day and through the evening.

At the end of the evening session, the host pastors found me and said, "Jeff, we saw you come in last night, but we've been so busy we weren't able to get to you."

I said, "No, I just got here this morning as I drove through the night to get here."

Jeff Jansen

They said, "We saw you last night in the balcony and acknowledged you from the pulpit."

I found that I ministered to over 50 people in Cincinnati on that Thursday night, while at the same time I was in another meeting in Nashville in the Glory of God. I was flabbergasted as I listened to reports of how I ministered to dozens of people that night.

Questions to Ponder

What would your response be if you had a similar bilocation experience?

_____

_____

_____

_____

_____

Would a measure of faith rise within you? Would you try to explain the event in logical terms?

_____

_____

_____

_____

_____

Who Was "the Man"?

Convulsionaires

There are two theories as to who "the Man" was that Thursday night. One is that it was in essence Jesus taking the face of a familiar friend and revealing His heart and intentions for an entire region. Another theory is based on the fact that I come from a line of revivalists and wonder-workers called the "Jansenists," who originated from Amsterdam, Holland.

"Jansenism" was founded in the early 17th century by Cornelius Jansen. One of the most remarkable displays of miraculous events ever recorded took place in Paris, precipitated by the death of a saintly and revered Jansenist deacon named Francois de Paris.

Cornelius Jansen

Because of Francois' saintly reputation, worshipers began to gather at his tomb, and a host of miraculous healings immediately were reported. The cured ailments included cancerous tumors, paralysis, deafness, arthritis, rheumatism, ulcerous sores, persistent fevers, prolonged hemorrhaging, and blindness. The mourners also started to experience strange, involuntary "spasms" or "convulsions." These convulsions quickly proved contagious, spreading until the streets were packed with men, women, and children, all twisting, turning, and shaking under the power of the Holy Spirit of God! Shakers and Quakers.

Dr. Middleton, in his book *Free Enquiry,* wrote that the evidence of these miracles is fully as strong as that of the wonders recorded of the apostles. The phenomena are among the most wonderful in history.

They're signs that make us wonder!

Whoever "the Man" was, something supernatural had occurred. I guess this is why these events are called signs and wonders. They're signs that make us wonder!

Question to Ponder

Which of the two "theories" presented do you believe took place? Explain your choice.

_____

_____

_____

_____

_____

_____

_____

Endnotes

1.   Joan Carroll Cruz, *Mysteries, Marvels, Miracles* (Rockford, IL: TAN Books and Publishers, Inc., 1997), 31-33.

2.   William Howitt, *The History of the Supernatural in All Ages and Nations and in All Churches* (London: Longman, Roberts and Green, 1863), 130-149.

FOR GROUP DISCUSSION

Have you experienced a singular moment that changed your life and/or ministry? What happened? In what way did it show the supernatural manifestation of God?

_____

_____

_____

_____

_____

_____

_____

_____

_____

Jeff Jansen has described different phenomena that have occurred to saints in the past and present. Is there one that you particularly believe God wants you to experience? Why?

_____

_____

_____

_____

_____

_____

_____

_____

LIFE APPLICATION

Bilocation may not have been something that you have ever considered as a possibility in your experience. For convenience sake, we may want to be in two places at once, but God uses bilocation for his purposes and not ours. Thinking through the ministry opportunities you currently have, how might God want to use this experience in your life?

_____

_____

_____

_____

_____

_____

_____

_____

_____

_____

_____

_____

_____

_____

_____

_____

GLORY RISING

Chapter 5

THE NEW GLORY REVIVAL

here are great destiny doors opening to the Church in this season offering new opportunities for spiritual advancement into the supernatural. We've had great forerunners who have imparted much to us, so we must get from them what was imparted. On January 16, 1956, William Branham prophesied, "America had turned down her opportunity with the Lord."

America missed her opportunity.

Because William Branham was the forerunning prophetic voice of the day, the tent revivals and the move of the Holy Spirit literally stopped. America missed her opportunity. She refused God's offer! The Lord told me in 2006 that He was offering the Church a "Golden Jubilee," as it marked the 50-year anniversary of Branham's word to the Church. This invitation must be understood and apprehended as we pass through the doors of destiny to encounter the Lord in genuine and experiential ways.

Question to Ponder

What are the signs of America's decision to "turn down her opportunity with the Lord"?

_____

_____

_____

_____

_____

_____

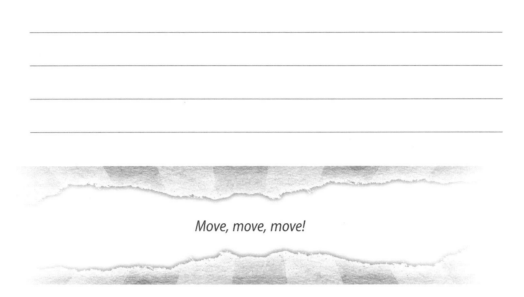

Move, move, move!

A Move of God Must Keep Moving

Many have been desperate for the new move of God. Those who seek the new will find the new. For a move of God to be a move of God, it has to keep moving. Many have become content

Bob Jones

with past revivals or moves, and when God begins to move again, they are simply satisfied with the level of anointing they have and never move on to the next level.

Bob Jones had an encounter with an angel who shouted at Bob: "Move, move, move! You tell the Church we'll be working with those who move in faith." In order to get Heaven and the angels to move with us, we must first move in faith.

Questions to Ponder

What does it mean when the author says that "many have been desperate for the new move of God"?

_____

_____

_____

_____

    What are the inward signs? What are the outward signs?

_____

_____

_____

_____

_____

_____

New Levels in the Glory

We must rise into the new levels of Glory. We must rise up into the new if we are to expect the new!

We must rise up into the new if we are to expect the new!

The Lord promises that if we will get up and begin to move into Him, His glory will rise on us, and we will shine and be radiant with His Glory (see Isa. 60:1). *"Then you shall see and be radiant, and your heart shall thrill and tremble with joy..."* (Isa. 60:5 AMP).

Questions to Ponder

    Are you hungry? Do you want to be *thrilled* and *tremble* with joy?

_____

_____

_____

_____

Get Ready

Get ready for new levels in the Glory of God like you have never experienced or heard of before. God is presenting this Glory revival in a way that will attract only the desperate and hungry. The hungry always seem to see what God is doing in the strangest of circumstances because their desire for Jesus causes them to look past the natural to see by the Spirit.

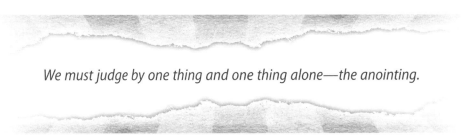

We must judge by one thing and one thing alone—the anointing.

As we move forward, we must judge by one thing and one thing alone—the anointing. This is the anointing of the Holy Spirit—allowing us to appraise things according to the Spirit and not a natural way of judging (see 1 Cor. 2:13-15). In this season we must fully embrace and experience the new waves of the Glory of God. The Glory will intensify as believers come together and bask in the awe of God's presence. The multitudes will come to the brightness of His shining.

Questions to Ponder

- Are you hungry for the new? Have you had enough of the status quo?

_____

_____

_____

_____

_____

- What does it mean when we're told that Jesus causes hungry people to look past the natural to see and appraise according to the Spirit?

_____

_____

_____

_____

_____

_____

Past Wonder-workers

Mystical wonder-workers of the past have revealed to us by their lives what is available now to an entire generation. Sons and daughters will be so transformed in their thinking about the power of God that signs, wonders, and miracles will become common occurrences—a natural part of life.

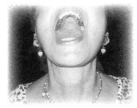

Gold Teeth

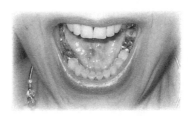

Gold Teeth

When the Israelites came out of the wilderness and entered the Promised Land, they had to shed one way of thinking for another because the wilderness paradigm no longer applied. It is a drastic change. It's a crossover of thoughts, a transformation of natural thought to spiritual thought, a coming out of an old wineskin and into a new, from a physical realm into a spiritual one.

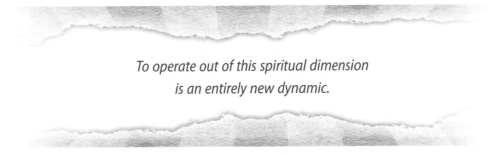

*To operate out of this spiritual dimension
is an entirely new dynamic.*

To operate out of this spiritual dimension, we have to leave our old way of thinking to see the Kingdom in operation. You can, if you walk in the laws of the Spirit. God is Spirit, and in Him we are spirit beings. The Church should be the answer the world is looking for. It is our right and place to do it. (See Isaiah 8:18-19.)

The Church has refused to be the supernatural door of information for the world.

God has placed it deep within humankind to seek direction from Him in the realm of the spirit. When satan stepped between God and humans in Eden, the flow of communion was severed (see 2 Cor. 4:4). He captured humankind's place in dominion as the "god of this world" and became the dictator of the atmosphere (see Eph. 2:2).

Jesus gave back to us the promise of Eden and the mandate of the Garden, which is *complete authority* over the wind, the seas, the animal kingdom, and everything in the earth (see Luke 10:19). This is our heritage and our inheritance.

Questions to Ponder

If someone asked what have you tasted of the good Word and the power of the Kingdom in your past, what would you say? What are you tasting currently?

_____

_____

_____

_____

_____

In what ways is God asking you to partner with Him?

_____

_____

_____

_____

_____

_____

_____

If the Church should be the answer the world is looking for, how are we to let them know we are the answer?

_____

_____

_____

_____

_____

_____

_____

_____

_____

_____

The Spirit of Sonship and Glory

When the Church understands who we are and who He is who lives in us, the world will see the mature Body of Jesus Christ in full operation. Just as Jesus moved on the earth 2,000 years ago, He will do more in these last days through a fully mature, corporately anointed Body of believers.

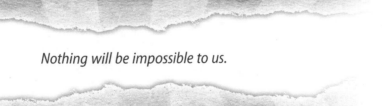

Nothing will be impossible to us.

It will be nothing less than Christ in us the hope of Glory. As we enter into this revelation as family—legal sons and daughters—nothing will be impossible for us. As we speak, our words will become *substance* in Glory, and matter will be created. All things are yours; you can do all things because hidden treasures of wisdom, knowledge, and revelation *are in* Jesus Christ, and are fully accessible to you.

Question to Ponder

How does the corporate anointing take place?

_____

_____

_____

_____

_____

_____

_____

_____

Transferred Into the Dominion of Light

What is your inheritance?

That you may walk (live and conduct yourselves) in a manner worthy of the Lord, fully pleasing to Him and desiring to please Him in all things, bearing fruit in every good work and steadily growing and increasing in and by the knowledge of God [with fuller, deeper, and clearer insight, acquaintance, and recognition] (Colossians 1:10 AMP).

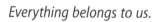

Everything belongs to us.

When you were born, your spiritual father was the prince of the power of the air (see Col. 1:12-13). Conceived in sin and born in sin, you were actually born spiritually dead. However, when you became born again, you were translated—the Father delivered and drew you to Himself. You could not do it. He carried you over from death into life (see Col. 1:14-16). Now everything belongs to us as joint heirs.

QUESTIONS FOR GROUP DISCUSSION

Do you want God no matter how He shows up? Will you choose not to be offended when He comes in a way you haven't expected? Qualify your answers to these questions.

_____

_____

_____

_____

Are you ready to be a sign and a wonder that topples the natural earthly order of things and contradicts the laws of physics? Do you want to be a son or a daughter who can command even hurricanes to stop and have them obey? Explain anything that might prevent you from this destiny.

_____

_____

_____

_____

"God has placed it deep within humankind to seek direction from Him in the realm of the spirit. Because the true children of light aren't providing the avenue for this to happen, the world has abandoned the truth for a counterfeit source." How do you think we can become this avenue?

_____

_____

_____

_____

LIFE APPLICATION

"Arise [...rise to new life]! Shine (be radiant with the glory of the Lord), for your light has come, and the glory of the Lord has risen upon you!" (Isa. 60:1 AMP). Do you see yourself as someone who is radiant with the Glory of the Lord?

_____

_____

_____

_____

_____

_____

_____

_____

_____

_____

_____

_____

_____

_____

_____

_____

_____

_____

_____

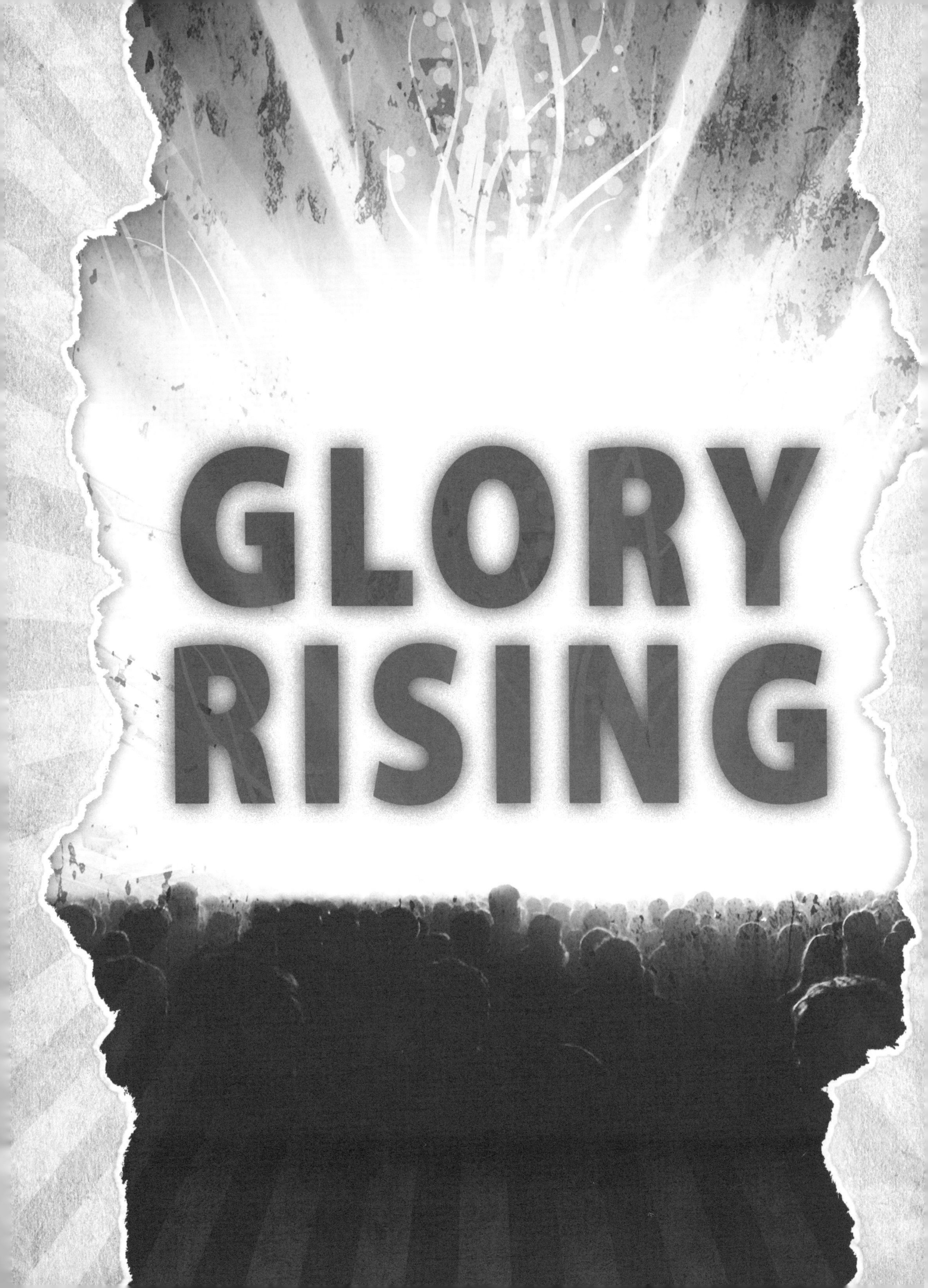
GLORY
RISING

Chapter 6

ACCELERATION IN THE GLORY

he power for acceleration is in the eternal, timeless realm of the Glory of God. When the realm of Glory moves into the realm of the natural, there comes a great acceleration for miracles, healings, signs, wonders, and the release of creative power.

It's essential that we first learn how to cultivate an atmosphere of God's presence in our individual lives through devotion, prayer, holiness, and humility. Second, we must learn how to corporately usher in the cloud of Glory through high praise, worship, and faith. And third, in order to step into maturity, we must learn how to operate in and from the realm of Glory. This means receiving revelation by faith through vision and imagination while in the Glory and also speaking and declaring the Word of God from the realm of Glory.

Questions to Ponder

Rate yourself in how well you cultivate an atmosphere of God's presence in your life through devotion, prayer, holiness, and humility. Which of these four is easiest for you? Which is most difficult to maintain?

_____

_____

_____

_____

_____

The Cloud of Glory and the Anointing

There is a difference between the anointing and the Glory. In the anointing, healings occur, but they are on an individual level. Through a gift of healing or the working of power, the minister prays for someone and he or she is healed; he is operating in the healing anointing, which covers him like a mantle, and he releases it to the people.

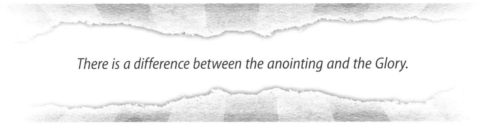

There is a difference between the anointing and the Glory.

The Glory cloud, however, is like a covering or a canopy that blankets the people; they all get touched. When the cloud of Glory is present, there is direct contact with Heaven—revelation increases, the seer realm is opened, gifts are activated, and miracles happen. The Glory of God is the manifest Presence and Person of the Lord Jesus Christ.

Questions to Ponder

How would you describe the difference between the anointing and the Glory?

_____

_____

_____

_____

_____

Have you experienced these realms? Were you able to distinguish the difference?

_____

_____

_____

_____

_____

_____

_____

Creative Power in the Realm of Glory

When God speaks, we become impregnated with His words. As time passes, that word grows and develops, eventually causing us to give birth to those specific promises. However, when God's word is spoken in the realm of Glory, the time it takes for the word to grow and mature is reduced to only a few moments—we see the promise instantly. This happens because the realm of Glory is the timeless, eternal realm where God is.

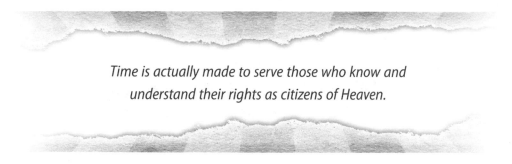

Time is actually made to serve those who know and
understand their rights as citizens of Heaven.

Healings happen over a period of time. Miracles, however, are instantaneous. Time is actually made to serve those who know and understand their rights as citizens of Heaven. When we experience the Glory realm, we are experiencing timelessness.

Vision, Imagination, and Faith

There are keys to unlock the realm of Glory, such as vision, imagination, and faith. Without faith we can't hear what God is saying. Imagination is one of the primary characteristics of the creative side of God. God imagined everything He created before He actually created it. To see into the realm of the supernatural, we must be able to envision, imagine, and perceive the realms of Glory through faith, which allows us to become intimately acquainted with Him and His ways.

Question to Ponder

Define vision, imagination, and faith. What is needed most in your life to grow in the realm of Glory?

_____

_____

_____

_____

_____

_____

_____

Worship and High Praises

When people begin to praise the Lord and give Him glory for the miracles, their faith level begins to rise. Faith and high praise will usher in the Glory cloud, creating an ideal atmosphere for greater miracles. As we step into the cloud of Glory, we are stepping into the realm of *all things are possible*. We need to worship God in the *now* and minister to Him in the *new*. We need fresh expectation—fresh faith.

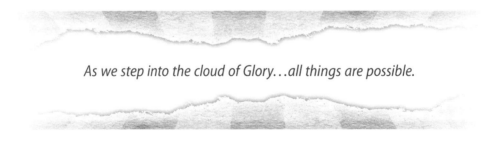

As we step into the cloud of Glory…all things are possible.

The Spirit Language of Heaven

We have access to God by faith. Faith is a higher law than the natural laws. By faith we can bypass space and time, stepping into the timeless realm. Faith is the door between the natural and supernatural dimensions. Faith operates from the Spirit of Revelation. Faith is the language that moves the realm of Glory.

When the Glory cloud appears, by faith we have the authority to decree, "Now!" and the substance from the supernatural realm will manifest and materialize in the natural. Faith is a higher law that exists out of time and operates from the law of higher truth not based on fact. The *truth* is by His stripes you are healed (see 1 Pet. 2:24), but the *fact* is you're sick. Which is dominant, truth or fact? Because truth is from the higher realm of God's presence and promise, it exceedingly triumphs over fact, human intellect, and reasoning—you are healed!

Question to Ponder

How does faith work as a door between the natural and supernatural dimensions?

_____

_____

_____

_____

_____

_____

_____

_____

New Faith Realms

In order for us to learn how to operate in the realm of Glory, we must understand about the realm of the spirit in correlation with the natural realm. The physical world was created and birthed from the spiritual realm. It's your spirit that receives revelation from the spirit realm. Supernatural substance is constantly being released between these two realms—both the natural and the spiritual.

In the natural world we learn by gathering information with our five senses. In the spirit realm we gain revelation with our spiritual senses. Revelation is nothing more than the revealed mechanics of God that enables us to think and operate from the supernatural dimension.

Questions to Ponder

What are the spiritual senses (as opposed to the five natural senses)? How do they work?

_____

_____

_____

_____

_____

_____

_____

God Is Creator

In order to experience creative power, it's important that we begin to see God as a "Creator God."

Jesus wanted His disciples to understand that He was the Word of power—He was Creator God. As they were on their way across the sea, Jesus revealed this to His disciples when He calmed the storm (see Mark 4:37-39). The disciples were amazed that even the wind and the sea obeyed Jesus. However, if they had possessed a revelation of God as Creator, they would have rebuked the wind and spoken to the sea themselves.

When we see God as Creator, we can get the faith we need for creative miracles. We see that, as children of God made in His image, creative miracles and healings should be normal occurrences, for we have His creative nature in us.

Healings Versus Creative Miracles

There is a difference between healings and creative miracles. According to Mark, one of the signs that follows believers is that *"…they will lay hands on the sick, and they* [the sick] *will recover"* (Mark 16:18). Recovery is the process of getting better over a period of time; it's not instantaneous or miraculous. Miracles, on the other hand, are instantaneous.

Miracles…are instantaneous.

When we are born again, we receive with the Spirit of God all of the DNA and genetics that He is. Paul says that we should not behave as mere men (see 1 Cor. 3:3). This is because we are far from being merely human—we are possessed by Creator God.

Questions to Ponder

Based on this chapter, why do you think we are not experiencing as many healings as God would desire?

_____

_____

_____

_____

_____

_____

Why aren't we seeing as many creative miracles as we should?

_____

_____

_____

_____

_____

_____

_____

The Power of Spoken Words

Jesus, as the Word, created all things. In this passage, the Greek word for "Word" is *logos*. Logos can also be interpreted into the English word *matter*. So we can say: "In the beginning was the 'Matter,' and the 'Matter' was with God, and the 'Matter' was God!"

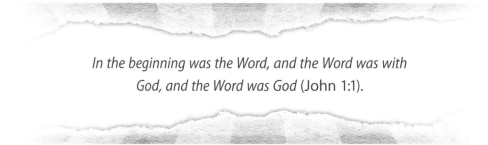

In the beginning was the Word, and the Word was with God, and the Word was God (John 1:1).

The spoken Word is Matter that creates substance. Therefore, we can see that words spoken in a faith decree come out as energized matter that materializes in the natural realm. When God spoke the worlds into being, all the frequencies of His Glory became manifest; the universe came into being (see Col. 1:16-17).

All Matter has Memory

When we understand by the spoken Word that we are being re-created in Christ now by His singing our song frequency, our intimacy with Him will change. His song of creation was not something He did 16 billion years ago. He is causing you to be now.

Matter has memory, and you can change everything that has been recorded by what you speak and observe, by the words you declare, or by the curses you remove and release in the name of Jesus. God wants us to participate with Him in releasing creative miracles.

Question to Ponder

Describe your understanding of the link between the spoken word and faith. What is the correlation between what you speak today and the past?

_____

_____

_____

_____

_____

_____

Releasing the New Song

Our worship is the key to bringing the new sounds and realms of Glory into the earth. It is the song of the Lord that flows from His heart through ours. As we join together and our worship intensifies, it will lift us into another realm—the Glory realm. Anyone can worship, but not everyone will worship with the new song of God. Until we sing the new song, the greater realm of the Spirit will not be released in our midst.

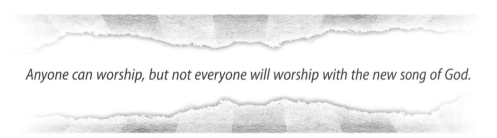

Anyone can worship, but not everyone will worship with the new song of God.

As we sing the new song, God releases His Word, which brings the framework of Heaven into the now. The superior realm of Heaven literally collides with the inferior, natural realm of earth, causing the inferior dimension to be instantly affected and changed.

Question to Ponder

Why do you think the new song is the catalyst for God to release His Word?

_____

_____

_____

_____

_____

_____

Our Commission

We are being commissioned by the Lord to step into new realms of Glory through worship and high praise. As we do this together, God's Kingdom is taking dominion upon the earth and is displacing every stronghold of the enemy. The doors of Heaven are opening wider than we've ever seen before, and we are witnessing the unfolding of the scrolls of destiny.

QUESTIONS FOR GROUP DISCUSSION

Describe the chain reaction that occurs between the new song, God's Word, the framework of Heaven, and the natural realm of the earth. How can you identify the new song?

_____

_____

_____

_____

_____

_____

_____

_____

Describe our commission of dominion and how it is obtained. What must you personally do to receive this commission to its fullest?

_____

_____

_____

_____

_____

_____

_____

_____

LIFE APPLICATION

Knowing that the spoken Word is Matter, how many words do you speak in faith in a single day that materialize in the natural realm? How can you increase in this dimension?

_____

_____

_____

_____

_____

_____

_____

_____

_____

_____

_____

_____

_____

_____

_____

_____

_____

_____

GLORY
RISING

Chapter 7

SOUND, LIGHT, AND THE POWER OF PRAISE

hanksgiving is key for releasing the Glory of God in our midst. The will of God for your life is that you give thanks for everything. Thanksgiving releases the Glory of God and the angels to work on your behalf.

Manifestations of Glory flow in abundance in an atmosphere supercharged with praise.

It is important for us to understand that attitudes shift our spiritual surroundings. Love, joy, peace, hate, jealousy, anger, and self-pity are not just attitudes, they are spirit and power in the emotions that harmonize the spirit and physical realms and generate substance. These attitudes are light that radiate out from us as a force with spiritual impact or vibration for both good and evil.

When God created the worlds, His voice was a vibration that formed the seen realm. These tiny atoms spin at their own intervals according to their own individual vibration or pattern. When Adam sinned, it wreaked such havoc in the physical world that the atoms were literally thrown out of whack, opening the door to demonic vibration from the kingdom of darkness. These demonic vibrations, in turn, brought sickness and disease into the habitable world, but the voice of God is still speaking. We can recreate the physical realm by framing it with the voice of faith.

Questions to Ponder

🌿　Matthew 6:10 tells us that it is the will of God to make earth look like Heaven. What do you think Heaven looks like?

_____

_____

_____

_____

_____

🌿　Why do you think that thanksgiving releases the Glory of God and the angels to work on your behalf?

_____

_____

_____

_____

_____

The Power of Thanksgiving

Science confirms that every created thing is made up of sound waves that are constantly spinning at different intervals, forming objects in matter of various densities both small and great. We also understand sound as a power that, when cranked up to a certain level or frequency, will crush glass or break windows in a house. All sound and color and images are wave lengths that move by vibration and are a power that have substance.

Every attitude carries its own power and vibration.

That being said, we need to understand that every attitude carries its own power and vibration that is recognizable in the realm of the spirit. It is not just an attitude—it is a force. This light force of vibration wraps itself around a person as if it were a coat or a jacket that continually pulls a person deeper into itself until he or she is completely taken over by it, whether for good or bad. Every attitude we release is filled with powerful vibrations wrapping themselves around us like a garment, further enveloping us into its cocoon-like power.

The words we wrap ourselves in will either set us free or imprison us here in this life and in eternity to come (see Matt. 12:37). There are spiritual repercussions to the words we release—both good and evil (see Prov. 18:21).

Your eye is the lamp of your body; when your eye (your conscience) is sound and fulfilling its office, your whole body is full of light; but when it is not sound and is not fulfilling its office, your body is full of darkness (see Luke 11:34 AMP). The individual that wraps himself in self-pity allows himself to be imprisoned by the power or force of that cloak of darkness (see Luke 11:34).

Jesus referred to this kind of light as "dark light." Every good or evil trait is not only a power, but it carries its own heavenly or demonic "tone" that is destructive or life-giving in nature. Depression carries with it a light that surrounds a person and is discernible in the realm of the spirit. Love, joy, and thanksgiving also have their own color and light with them that attract the angelic realm from the Kingdom of light.

If we can learn to recognize these truths, we can change our circumstances by putting off the old nature with its attitudes, cravings, lusts, and appetites and by choice put on the Lord Jesus Christ and the new heavenly nature of love, joy, and peace, which is born from above. By doing this we can break the power and magnetic attraction of demonic darkness and attract Heaven and the angelic realm of light.

Questions to Ponder

Have you ever seen "tones" in someone's character traits before you ever knew them? Why is this possible?

_____

_____

_____

_____

How will putting off our old nature change our circumstances?

_____

_____

_____

_____

_____

_____

_____

_____

The Garment of Praise

Isaiah prophesied to a generation that was yet to come. He said to put on the garment of praise for the spirit of heaviness (see Isa. 61:3). The Hebrew word for "garment" is a *mattah,* which means to "wrap oneself in or to veil oneself." When we choose to put on the garment of praise, we begin to wrap ourselves in the power and light of that garment, which destroys the spirit of heaviness.

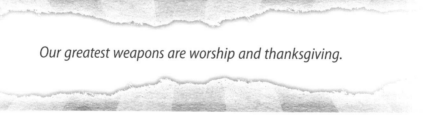

Our greatest weapons are worship and thanksgiving.

The Hebrew word for "praise" is *hallal,* which means to *"shine forth* with *sound* and *color."* When we begin to praise, we shine with *light* and *color.* So when we choose to praise, we wrap ourselves in a supernatural heavenly garment of power and light that flows with an unstoppable force that destroys the spirit of heaviness. When we choose to be thankful, we are filled with light, and we put off the power of sadness and despair and dismantle the realm of the demonic.

With our attitudes we are constantly attracting one of two kingdoms—either the Kingdom of light or the kingdom of darkness. Our greatest weapons are worship and thanksgiving.

Questions to Ponder

Why is it true that when we choose to put on the garment of praise we begin to wrap ourselves in power and light?

_____

_____

_____

_____

_____

If it is true that we are constantly attracting either the Kingdom of light or the kingdom of darkness with our attitudes, what kingdom are you attracting at this very moment? Why?

_____

_____

_____

_____

_____

_____

The High Praises of God

Praise will bind the kings with chains and nobles with fetters of iron (see Ps. 149:1-9). Who are these kings and nobles? They are both the natural and demonic kings of Heaven and earth. When the high praises of God are in our mouths, the two-edged sword is automatically in our hands, wreaking vengeance upon all of our enemies. Sickness, disease, depression, oppression, cancer, and every enemy against God's people will flee in the presence of a praising, thankful people. Satan can't stand the Glory of God. Praise and thanksgiving have always been the weapons of choice for God's people (see 2 Cor. 10:4-5).

Satan can't stand the Glory of God.

By putting on the clothing of light and power in thanksgiving and praise, we are able to destroy and overthrow wrong mind-sets and negative thinking that keep us bound in our present condition and circumstances. We are told to praise and thank God in every situation, regardless of how difficult it is, because it's God's will for us (see 1 Thess. 5:18).

Unless we get this understanding, we cannot go any further in God. We will be held captive and unable to break through the veil of darkness to get into the realm of light where God wants us to be. When we are manifesting thanksgiving and praise, it releases a power that will transform us and heal us—body, soul, and spirit.

Question to Ponder

If we believe that praise binds kings and nobles, how can our praise do more to change our governmental leaders than protests or even letter-writing campaigns?

_____

_____

_____

_____

Attracting Heaven

When we manifest faith, we are emitting a power and a brilliance that will attract Heaven. Praise is a glorious golden light that manifests in the realm of the spirit. When we are thankful, it opens up the gates of Heaven for everything we have need of. When we moan and grumble about things in our lives, it attracts a demonic power that will cut us off from Heaven and eventually will even affect the cells in our bodies and the marrow in our bones.

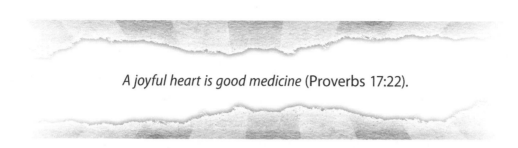

A joyful heart is good medicine (Proverbs 17:22).

Sickness is a vibration that works against the body and causes it to decompose. Faith and thanksgiving are powerful vibrations that destroy sickness when exercised. When we choose to be thankful, a heavenly glorious light and power will fill us and transform us right down to the cells in our body. You may feel sick, but stop energizing the sickness by talking about it. Thank God for all the good things in your life and forget sickness and it will die. Give thanks to God in everything and in every situation, and watch your circumstances instantly change. Watch your body gain new strength and power.

Questions to Ponder

How much time do you spend "venting" to others? Does this behavior help or harm you? Explain.

_____

_____

_____

_____

_____

Do you truly believe your circumstances can instantly change if you give thanks to God in everything and in every situation? Why or why not?

_____

_____

_____

_____

_____

What Are We Manifesting?

When we begin to praise God, we immediately become surrounded with heavenly light and the Glory. The spirit world knows who we are not just by our words, but also by the color of light that emanates from us. These attitudes are a power that pours from us and opens up gates that will take us deeper into the emotion and the spirit of an attitude, good or bad. It is clearly, then, our responsibility in everything to overcome with a right attitude and a thankful heart. What we manifest in attitude and atmosphere will reproduce around us. Happiness is a choice. We choose to produce joy or depression. Which cloak will you wear today?

QUESTIONS FOR GROUP DISCUSSION

We can "recreate the physical by framing it with the voice of faith." What does this mean to you?

_____

_____

_____

_____

_____

_____

_____

Have you found it to be true that every attitude you release is filled with power vibrations wrapping themselves around you like a garment? If this principle is true, what must you do to be sure you wrap yourself with the right garment?

_____

_____

_____

_____

_____

_____

_____

LIFE APPLICATION

According to Matthew 12:37, how are you wrapping yourself today—in freedom or imprisonment? How does what you wrap around yourself today affect your eternity?

_____

_____

_____

_____

_____

_____

_____

_____

_____

_____

_____

_____

_____

_____

_____

_____

_____

_____

GLORY RISING

Chapter 8

THE TREE OF LIFE

In the beginning, Adam walked in the Garden of Eden with the Lord, who was the life of Adam. The Lord freely gave Adam all things in the Garden, including free access to the Tree of Life, which he ate from daily. Adam's sin severed his communion with the Lord. (See Genesis 2:9; 3:22; 2:24.)

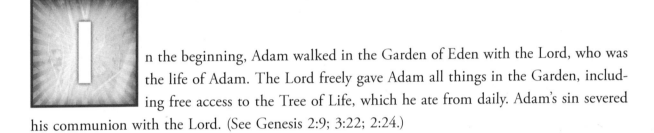

The fruit of the Tree of Life is God's unconditional love.

Through the Cross, access to the presence of God was gained for all who believed. The Tree of Life was again available to humankind (see Rev. 2:7; 22:14). The *fruit* of the Tree of Life is God's unconditional love, and it's for our healing *now* because we will not need healing in Heaven.

Question to Ponder

Why do you think God determined to make Adam dependent upon Him to live?

_____

_____

_____

_____

_____

To the Overcomers

In the Book of Revelation, we see the Tree of Life in the Garden in the beginning in Genesis and that same Tree of Life at the end of all things in Revelation 22.

There were two trees in the beginning of time—the Tree of Life and the Tree of the Knowledge of Good and Evil. The Tree of the Knowledge of Good and Evil essentially represented human ability to know right and wrong in the natural, completely independent of God.

The Tree of Life represented relationship with the Lord and dependence on Him. One tree represented independence; the other tree represented relationship and dependence upon the Lord, who is the Way, the Truth, and the Life. One required humans to live by their soul, and the other required them to live by their spirit.

Questions to Ponder

How often do you seem to run to the Tree of the Knowledge of Good and Evil and rely on your own abilities and knowledge rather than eating from the Tree of Life? Why does it seem easier sometimes to run to the wrong tree?

_____

_____

_____

_____

_____

Spiritual Life

The Tree of Life offered spiritual life for Adam and was the life-giving flow of supernatural connection between Heaven and earth. When Adam took of the wrong tree, he exercised his free will, and in this fallen state of his knowledge of evil, innocence was lost. If he had taken of the Tree of Life in this fallen state, he would have lived forever as a fallen man. This is why the Lord God had to put Adam and Eve out of the Garden of Eden, even placing two angels there to guard access to "the Way" to the Tree of Life.

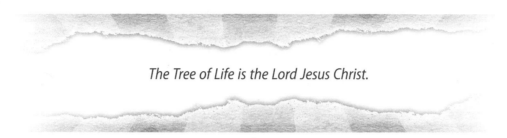

The Tree of Life is the Lord Jesus Christ.

The Tree of Life is now in Heaven (see Rev. 2:7). This Tree of Life is the Lord Jesus Christ. It says those *who overcome* will have access to this Tree of Life. When the overcomers eat of the tree, they will live forever (see Rev. 2:7; 22:2; 22:14).

Jesus said that we were to dwell in Him and that He would dwell in us (see John 15:4-5). We have the awesome privilege of becoming a branch of this Tree who is the Lord Jesus Christ, and this Tree is for the healing of the nations. The only way we can bear fruit is to abide in Him. This lasting fruit is for the healing of the nations.

Questions to Ponder

Have you ever considered yourself grafted to the Tree of Life? Have you ever thought of what fruit you are able to produce because you are grafted into that Tree?

_____

_____

_____

_____

_____

Life-giving River of Love

This life-giving river is a pure river of love, and that love becomes incredible light that has the power to heal, to restore, and to transform. It becomes a river of the love of God, and when we drink of it, we become beings of light, dispersing and flowing in light.

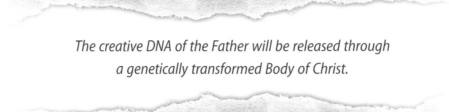

*The creative DNA of the Father will be released through
a genetically transformed Body of Christ.*

The creative DNA of the Father will be released through a genetically transformed Body of Christ that moves and flows in the currents of love. Creative miracles and supernatural ability will be the distinguishing mark of those who have been transformed by this power of light and love. Even creation will see it and respond to it.

Questions to Ponder

What is flowing out of you? What *kind* of light is flowing out of you? Is it a bright, brilliant light or a dim, dark light?

_____

_____

_____

_____

_____

_____

Angels Guard the "Way"

Two cherubim guarded the entrance to the Garden of Eden—the "Way" to "the Tree of Life" after the expulsion of Adam and Eve (see Gen. 3:24). Cherubim are winged angelic creatures. God instructed Moses to make two cherubim out of hammered gold on the top of the two ends of the mercy seat on the Ark of the Covenant. They were to have their wings spread upward, overshadowing the cover with them, facing each other, and looking toward the cover, according to Exodus 25:18-20.

The cover was the mercy seat and signified "atonement" or "covering." Jesus died on the Cross and the veil was rent, giving us *access* to the mercy seat. The "Way" to the mercy seat was opened up to humanity again because God so loved the world. The love of God opened the lid to the manna of the Tree of Life—that hidden manna, Christ Jesus.

The Light of Love

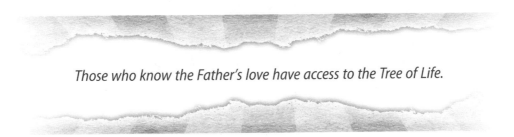

Those who know the Father's love have access to the Tree of Life.

God will have a people who are trees of righteousness in the last days. If you desire to be one of those, then you must abide in, walk in, and bear the fruit of love for transformation. When love flows from you, it is transformed into a power of light. When love turns into light and the light passes through you, you will experience that healing and transformation. In that light are healing, revelation, knowledge, understanding, and insight. Flowing from your mind and your lips will be love. How vital is this way of love in your life? Those who know the Father's love have access to the Tree of Life. Jesus said He is the "Way," the "Truth," and the "Life." He is the Way to life eternal. We must eat of His body and drink of His blood, for He is the great Tree of Life—our Life Source.

Questions to Ponder

How has Jesus opened up the way for you to access the Tree of Life? Have you grown in producing the fruit of love since you first came to know Christ?

_____

_____

_____

_____

_____

_____

Power of Communion

We are being cemented into Christ—His nature in our nature. In order for us to move into the next season, we must first come to know and practice *the lasting value and power of communion.*

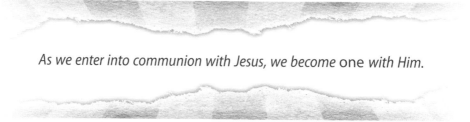

As we enter into communion with Jesus, we become one *with Him.*

The word *communion* has to do with *communication*—Jesus speaks and we listen; we speak, He listens. As we enter into communion with Jesus we become *one* with Him. We actually become partakers of life because He is Life. We are set free from the *law of sin and death* by the *Spirit of Life* through our identification with the *resurrection* and *ascension* of Jesus.

A Life-giving Spirit

Jesus said that He came that we might have life and have it *more abundantly* (see John 10:10). We become partakers of the *law of the Spirit* through our identification with Him as a life-giving Spirit. When this happens, we don't just receive life in our spirits and minds, but in our physical bodies as well.

> *...unless you eat the flesh of the Son of Man and drink His blood, you have no life in yourselves. This is the bread which came down out of Heaven; not as the fathers ate and died; he who eats this bread will live forever* (John 6:53,58).

Jesus was offering them a higher life in which they would not die—bread from Heaven that gives eternal life.

Questions to Ponder

- What is the difference between the bread of earth and the bread of Heaven? How do we partake of the bread of Heaven?

_____

_____

_____

_____

_____

The Right to Eat

Those who overcome have access to eat from the Tree of Life in the Paradise of God. Once again we see that we have access to the Tree of Life, to the Bread of Life, to abundant life, to eternal life through the broken body and shed blood of Jesus Christ. When we partake of communion, the way to the Tree of Life is opened to us—we have access to His resurrection power and life. As we take communion, we see bread, but Jesus said it was His body. As we take the cup, we see the fruit of the vine, but Jesus said it was His blood. Having the mind of a child, we simply believe what Jesus said—not what we see.

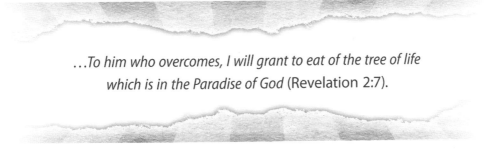

...To him who overcomes, I will grant to eat of the tree of life which is in the Paradise of God (Revelation 2:7).

Living in the Glory of God

When God led the children of Israel out of Egyptian slavery and through the desert, there was not a single feeble person among them. They were supernaturally sustained in the Glory of God. As long as they ate the bread that came from Heaven, their bodies, clothing, shoes, and all they possessed did not corrupt or age. The molecular structure of all they owned and possessed was kept new and fresh. As they ate the bread of angels, they were kept from sickness (see Ps. 78:25).

Just as Adam needed to come to the Tree of Life to eat and live, we must do the same. When we partake of the Tree of Life, we will live the fullness of time that has been given to us. People are looking beyond liturgical religious forms—pressing past routine worship into a spiritual reality. There is a fresh hunger for the living God. By faith believers are pressing through by partaking of the flesh and blood of Jesus—eating from the Tree of Life.

QUESTIONS FOR GROUP DISCUSSION

What does the act of partaking of communion mean to you? How does it affect your walk with God?

_____

_____

_____

_____

_____

_____

_____

_____

_____

Have you ever imagined living in the Glory of God where nothing decays, ages, or becomes corrupted? Why didn't such an experience sustain Israel's faith in God during their desert wanderings?

_____

_____

_____

_____

_____

_____

_____

_____

LIFE APPLICATION

The Tree of Life is distinctly different from the Tree of the Knowledge of Good and Evil. What reminders must you give yourself to stop partaking from the wrong tree? Is there something you can do today to bring yourself to the Tree of Life in a tangible way?

_____

_____

_____

_____

_____

_____

_____

_____

_____

_____

_____

_____

_____

_____

_____

_____

_____

_____

GLORY RISING

Chapter 9

SUPERNATURAL PATHWAYS

There is a strong emphasis coming into the Body of Christ in this next season of time that will quickly become the hallmark theme of everything that we as believers are to become. This Kingdom reality is the cornerstone of truth that will anchor the Church of Jesus Christ to its original mandate, propelling the Church into a reawakening of sonship marked by powerful displays of the miraculous. This will in turn lead to the beginning of transformation of churches, cities, regions, and whole nations. This reawakening is Christ in us, the hope of Glory (see Eph. 4:12-13; Gal. 4:19).

Question to Ponder

Explain the previous paragraph in your own words, using your own life experiences as an illustration. What are you seeing that affirms the statements?

_____

_____

_____

_____

_____

_____

_____

Little "god" Man

Adam was born from Creator God with His likeness and ability in the earth. If the prevailing law of creation is that everything brings forth after its own kind, then what was Adam really like? What kind of son did God actually bring forth? More importantly, what was it that was really lost in the Garden of Eden, and what was it that Jesus Christ came to restore to us? To answer this more fully, let's look at an encounter that Jesus had with the Jewish leaders of His day. They asked Him to tell them plainly if He was indeed the Christ, and Jesus answered them like this.

Men are called gods.

"I and the Father are One." Again the Jews brought up stones to stone Him. Jesus said to them, "My Father has enabled Me to do many good deeds. [I have shown many acts of mercy in your presence] [supernatural acts of miracles]. For which of these do you mean to stone Me?" The Jews replied, "We are not going to stone You for a good act [for doing supernatural acts], but for blasphemy, because You, a mere Man, make Yourself [out to be] God. Jesus answered, "Is it not written in your Law, 'I said, You are gods'? So men are called gods [by the law], men to whom God's message came—and the Scripture cannot be set aside or cancelled or broken or annulled" (John 10:30-35 AMP).

Did you hear what Jesus said? He said, "Men are called gods. To these men God's message came, and the Scripture cannot be set aside, or cancelled, or broken, or annulled."

In essence Jesus was saying to them, "Why do you accuse Me of acting like God when we are all His earthly representatives and are to act on God's behalf? Should we not all be doing great works of power since God has given the earth to man to rule as little 'gods'?" (see Ps. 115:16; 82:1,6).

Jesus was quoting Psalm 82:6, saying that we are gods (small "g"). We are God's "creator gods" on the earth, establishing His earthly government as ambassadors of His supernatural Kingdom. Jesus and the Father are One. He is the outshining of His Glory, the projection of the invisible God—and we are imago deo, made in His image and likeness. As we abide in Him and He in us, we have access into the heavens and are able to move in power and authority on the earth (see John 1:12).

Jesus didn't shed His blood on the Cross just so we could go to Heaven when we die. He has restored to us the long-lost relationship title deed of "Sons of God." We must understand that man was not created simply to serve, but to be the "gods of this world." God longs for us to begin to understand His nature and His ways. He wants us to take dominion over the elements, sin, sickness, disease, and death, exercising our God-given authority.

When I believe that I possess His Spirit, I am able to administrate His dominion—I have something tangible that I can give. The same Spirit that raised Christ from the dead dwells in me. We are joint heirs to the throne with Jesus—we have something to give away.

Questions to Ponder

What is the difference between people being created in the image of God as a god *(elohim)* on earth and the way in which humanism has made humanity into their own gods?

_____

_____

_____

_____

_____

What title deed was restored to you when you accepted Jesus' gift of salvation? How does this deed create a difference in your life right now rather than just in the by and by?

_____

_____

_____

_____

_____

Branded Sons of God

When Paul wrote to the church at Ephesus and Galatia telling them that his intention for them was the perfecting and full equipping of the saints until they arrived at really mature manhood, he was bearing all of the history and design of humanity in mind. Paul was telling them in Galatians 4:19 that he was actually suffering birth pangs in himself until Christ was completely and permanently formed, or molded, within them.

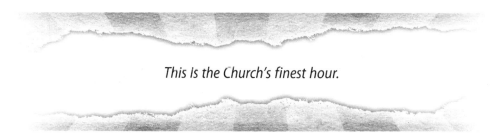

This Is the Church's finest hour.

There is a maturing taking place—a coming to fullness of all things, both good and evil. We are at the end of the age, and the seeds of the Kingdom sown in our hearts are coming to age and maturity. The things we have known in a limited measure will be made fully known. This reawakening Body of Christ is coming forth in the full power of Heaven and will fill the whole earth with the knowledge of the Glory of God. This is the Church's finest hour. God always saves the best for last, and this shining forth will be none other than *Christ in us,* the hope of Glory (see Col. 1:27).

Question to Ponder

Read Galatians 4:19. How do we have Christ completely and permanently formed, or molded, within us?

_____

_____

_____

_____

_____

_____

Ancient Pathways and Spirit Travel

The Bible is clear that there are roads that lead to eternal paths, and we are to ask the Lord for them to lead us in the good, old way. These ancient pathways were established at the creation of the world and are meant for us to walk so we can find rest for our souls.

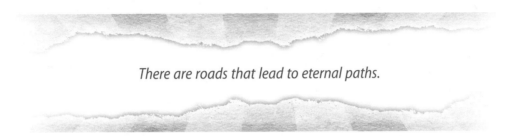

There are roads that lead to eternal paths.

Transportations and translocations are divine acts of God that physically or spiritually move an individual into different places in this time or another. Peter was in a secure prison and was delivered from jail by an angel that opened a portal in the spirit realm and led him outside. Jesus transported a whole boat with His disciples in it to the other side of the sea after He came walking to them on the water.

Supernatural transportation or translocation comes through union with God, birthed from a holy desperation to know the limitless measures of His Kingdom.

In spirit travel there is a special faith, anointing, and protection placed around the individual so that person can perform what the Lord is leading him or her to do. When an out-of-the-body experience takes place, the person's spirit literally leaves the physical body and travels in the spirit world by the Spirit of the Lord. The surrounding environment appears different, as that person is seeing in the spirit and not the natural. The Lord directs our eyes to see what He wants us to see. Ezekiel had many experiences like this (see Ezek. 3:14; 8:1-3; 37:1; 43:5).

Interior Graces of Prayer

The out-workings of the miraculous in transportations and heavenly encounters are a wonder and are awesome in themselves. But these spiritual dimensions are only possible through the outer workings of the *interior graces* of prayer. Transformation of the mind and the spirit of people through communion with God is crucial. In order for the outward to manifest the Kingdom of God, there needs to be the complete possessing of the inward parts of people. This comes about not by under-standing or by reason, but rather by self-abandonment and the complete overtaking of the Holy

Spirit in an individual's life. Deep prayer and communion with God are the catalysts for Heaven to open up and for the experience of supernatural encounters.

Question to Ponder

What is the "outer workings of the interior graces of prayer"?

_____

_____

_____

_____

_____

_____

Angels That Assist

Angels are most often involved in supernatural encounters, acting as agents between God and humans. Often they will bring instructions and direction in these experiences. Angels are mighty and powerful heavenly beings. They are the messengers of God. Their main duty is to worship God and also to see that the instructions of God are carried out. They patrol the earth. They help, protect, and minister to God's people. They carry out most of the activities between Heaven and the believers, and sometimes they even appear to unbelievers. They are very strong, intelligent, obedient, and swift. They can reach any part of the universe in seconds. One angel can also kill hundreds of thousands of human beings in just one night (see 2 Kings 19:35-36).

Daniel understood the operations of the angels. He knew that God could shut the mouths of lions (see Dan. 6:16-32). God sent His angel to shut the mouths of lions. One angel shut the mouths of many lions. That is just how powerful angels are. You may not need many. Just one is enough to silence all your enemies.

David also knew how the angels fight for God's people (see Ps. 35:4-6; 34:7).

The activities of the angels are everywhere in the Bible from Genesis to Revelation—only a few were mentioned where they fought on behalf of the children of God. Prayer warriors and indeed all Christians should take advantage of this great weapon that God has graciously made available to us.

QUESTIONS FOR GROUP DISCUSSION

Have you ever felt or seen an angel move on your behalf? Or do you personally know someone who has had an encounter with an angel? What is your understanding/experience of how angels work for us?

_____

_____

_____

_____

_____

_____

_____

_____

Do you think this is the Church's "finest hour"? What will mark this increase in activity if the world is to believe our message?

_____

_____

_____

_____

_____

_____

_____

_____

LIFE APPLICATION

Your testimony is your living witness of God's forgiveness and grace in your life. Do you also have a testimony of God's miraculous power? Do you have an experience of God's creative encounters that might give faith to another person?

_____

_____

_____

_____

_____

_____

_____

_____

_____

_____

_____

_____

_____

_____

_____

_____

_____

_____

GLORY RISING

Chapter 10

UNHOLY PATHWAYS
OF THE OCCULT

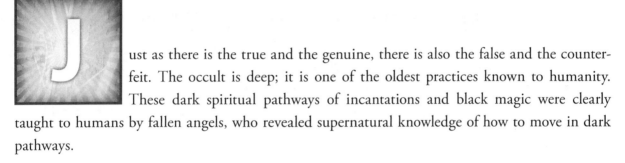ust as there is the true and the genuine, there is also the false and the counterfeit. The occult is deep; it is one of the oldest practices known to humanity. These dark spiritual pathways of incantations and black magic were clearly taught to humans by fallen angels, who revealed supernatural knowledge of how to move in dark pathways.

I want to reveal details of occult activity, not as a means of glorifying it, but rather to reveal the hidden design and nature of humanity as God-created supernatural beings. If the fallen, unregenerate person can move with powerful demonstrations in dark supernatural ability, what do we as blood-bought, Spirit-filled believers have access to by the Holy Spirit of God?

Questions to Ponder

In your understanding, what is a "dark pathway"? How do they work against the purposes of God?

_____

_____

_____

_____

_____

_____

Occult activities and supernatural experiences are counterfeits; what does this mean?

_____

_____

_____

_____

_____

_____

Shape-shifters and Transcended Physics

Were-cults (werewolves)—like their aquatic *mere*-cult or "mermaid" counterparts—are based on establishing human partnerships with certain kinds of evil spirits. These spirits have powers to manipulate physical realities and transcend the natural laws of physical matter that we consider to be normal.

…the hidden design and nature of humanity as God-created supernatural beings.

The entire sphere of the "miraculous" is dubbed such based on an established experience that contradicts our narrow understanding of the laws that govern the physical realm. Scriptural accounts of animals talking, axe heads floating on water, men possessed by superhuman powers carrying off the fortified gates of an entire city, prophets taking trips in the spirit world, or angels appearing out of nowhere taking on a physical form and then engaging in physical activities (such as eating and drinking)—all are such examples of transcended physics.

Scripture also records the involvement of "incubus" spirits making their bid to defile the human race and corrupt humankind's lineage (see Gen. 6:1-7). This was a diabolical attempt to prevent the "seed of woman" from ever bruising satan's head and fulfilling the Edenic prophecy of Genesis 3:15. In these and similar instances, the spirits involved were fallen, evil spirits who still retained these special powers but now employed them in service to satan rather than to Christ, the Lord of Hosts.

These spirits are behind the pervasive stories, legends, and cultural beliefs of were- and mere-beasts (werewolves and mermaids).

Questions to Ponder

What is your experience thus far with supernatural events? Why do you think it's possible for people who aren't followers of Christ to move in the supernatural?

_____

_____

_____

_____

_____

_____

The Kingdom of Darkness

It is a very common practice in the satanic kingdom to use demonic means to be able to move from one place to another. You see this practice in witchcraft, occultism, and in the false religions. It is often used by agents of darkness for various purposes, which include attending demonic meetings and going to execute evil assignments.

In fact, almost all witches, advanced occultists, and their counterparts in false religions have this demonic ability. Remember that it is the same spirit—satan—that is working in them. For them to be efficient, they must be able to move supernaturally from one location to another. I know a man who travels abroad by going into a coffin placed in his "secret" room. There is also a blind native doctor (occultist) whom I know very well who has the ability to go into the water and stay for months in the marine kingdom. He is a very strong agent of that dark kingdom.

The church must arise from slumber.

There are others who vanish when faced with any serious danger. They wear amulets (rings, waistbands, handkerchiefs, necklaces, etc.) or make incisions on their bodies that give them the power to effectively remove themselves from any point of danger to a safer place, especially when the situation is a life-threatening one. You find these kinds of people in the military and police and among politicians, and many others in society.

There are a lot of high demonic manipulations going on in the kingdom of darkness. It is very true that the human agents of the satanic kingdom can travel to any part of the world and even to the planets without using any physical means of transportation.

Yes, agents of satan possess illegal supernatural powers, and they are common these days. This is the reason why the Church must rise from slumber.

Questions to Ponder

Why does Jeff Jansen, the author, call the powers of satan and his agents "illegal supernatural powers"? What is illegal about them?

_____

_____

_____

_____

_____

Two Sources of Power

When Moses had Aaron throw down his rod, it became a snake (see Exod. 7:10). The sorcerers also had rods that duplicated the same sign, only notice that the Word says that Moses' *rod*, not snake, swallowed up their rods (see v. 12)! The rod is symbolic of authority. The Bible says, *"They [those who overcome] will rule the nations with an iron rod..."* (Rev. 2:27 NLT). All the magicians had rods, but that day they went home "rod-less," for the authority of Moses swallowed up theirs. God is introducing us again to the supernatural dimension, but remember that lucifer said in Isaiah 14:14, *"I will...be **like** the Most High."* As with Moses, so it is with us that God's supernatural reality will overcome satan's counterfeit.

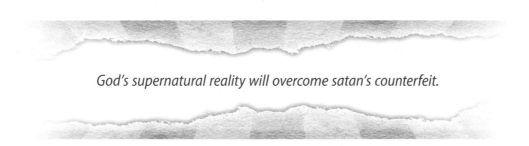

God's supernatural reality will overcome satan's counterfeit.

We as believers are dependent upon the Spirit of God, and witches are dependent upon demons and cycles of nature. For them, there are hindrances in performing certain rituals, based on the wrong time in the lunar cycle, the wrong pronunciation of a word in an incantation, or a lack of a pre-ritual meditation. For us, the more childlike our faith becomes, the more we open up to our Father doing things in and through us that we hadn't even thought of before.

Witchcraft is another spirit the devil has released to destroy humankind and to battle the Church. This spirit is the most wicked of all spirits in the kingdom of darkness. All it wants to achieve is destruction. You will always know its operations when you see manipulation, intimidation, and domination. It will always want to control no matter the cost. Witches are always afraid of midnight warriors. Though the strong ones will attempt to resist or even counter your attack, if you persist, they will ultimately bow.

Who is a witch? A witch is a person, male or female, who is possessed by the spirit of witchcraft—a person who uses magic, charms, or spiritual powers for evil purposes.

Witches normally meet in their covens (their spiritual meeting places) between midnight and 3:00 A.M. and sometimes beyond. Witches can turn into different forms when they go on operations or meetings. They can turn into birds, cats, owls, rats, cockroaches, vultures, snakes, etc. It depends on their assignments and situation. They usually turn into the forms that will help them gain entrance or achieve their particular objective in an operation. As I was putting this work together, I heard on the radio about a woman caught in the middle of the night by a trap set for the antelopes in the forest. When her captors asked her how she came into the trap, she confessed to being a witch. In Lagos, Nigeria, on many occasions large birds have fallen from the sky, only to turn into human beings. I have even read a narrative by a very powerful, respected Pentecostal minister in Lagos telling how a witch was drawn down from the sky by their prayer force. She fell right there in their church premises and was pleading for mercy!

These things are not really strange to Africans or in some other places where the forces of darkness still reign. The dominant spirits you encounter in these places are marine spirits and the spirit of witchcraft, and these have also invaded churches. They are even moving into the house of God, causing much havoc to the believers and the Body of Christ. Their objective is to work against the plan of God. The Church must wake up and battle these wicked spirits. We must break their strongholds and set the captives free.

Question to Ponder

🍃 From the information given that witches normally meet between midnight and 3:00 A.M., what emphasis of purpose does that give all-night prayer vigils and praying before you sleep?

_____

_____

_____

_____

_____

Powers in the Waters

There are also great powers and demonic activities from the waters. These we often refer to as the marine powers or spirits or "mere-spirits."

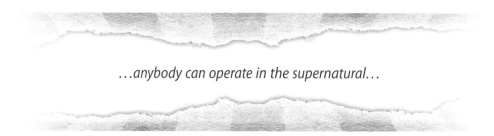

…anybody can operate in the supernatural…

They are the spirits you see most often in the course of deliverance ministry in Africa, India, and other places. These marine spirits also manipulate and use humans. They operate mostly through physical and spiritual activities and sacrifices. People worship these demons for power, wealth, and protection. I know people who serve these demons that go into the water (rivers and seas) and stay for several months. These wicked spirits cause most of the accidents on our waterways and even roads. We must pray for their downfall and stop their activities against human beings and the work of God. These stories cause us to understand that *anybody* can operate in the supernatural, but only blood-bought, Spirit-filled sons and daughters have the legal right to do so.

QUESTIONS FOR GROUP DISCUSSION

Have you or anybody in your family (that you know) entertained any activity within the occult world? If so, have you confronted this activity, renounced it, and replaced it with the Holy Spirit's power?

_____

_____

_____

_____

_____

_____

_____

_____

Are you afraid of occult activity? Why or why not? Does your mind-set embrace the dark pathways that the author explains? Does your heart ring with assurance as to the victory you have over darkness?

_____

_____

_____

_____

_____

_____

_____

LIFE APPLICATION

As you open yourself to the possibility of the supernatural ability that has been placed within you by God, how will you safeguard yourself against the illegal activity of satan and his agents?

_____

_____

_____

_____

_____

_____

_____

_____

_____

_____

_____

_____

_____

_____

_____

_____

_____

_____

_____

GLORY RISING

Chapter 11

THE SPIRIT OF MAN

ho are we? Sages, philosophers, theologians, and curious people throughout the ages of time have asked this question. David asked that very question of God as he considered God's handiwork in creation (see Ps. 8:4-8):

What is man that You take thought of him?

It is a good question and one that begs an answer. "Why are we here? Where did we come from? How old are we?" Indeed, we live on a planet spinning in infinite space—why are we here? We all seek answers to these questions, at least in part. Let's discover what the Bible has to say about these perplexing inquiries.

What Is Man?

We already know through reading Genesis 1:26-27 that we are made in the image and likeness of God. Not only do we have the same shape and form as God, but we also have similar faculties of mind, will, and emotion. Essentially, though, we are spirit. The Scriptures refer often to humans as spirit; this is the first truth we should grasp (see 1 Cor. 2:11; Prov. 20:27).

God gave us a calling and purpose before we were born into this world and before the world was created—before time even (see 2 Tim. 1:9). We were in Him as members of Him, represented by Him, united to Him, and we were blessed in Him with all spiritual blessings.

Question to Ponder

How does knowing that your spirit has existed far before you were born create a fresh view of yourself while on earth?

_____

_____

_____

_____

_____

Astounding Truth

In the first 37 chapters of the Book of Job, he complained about his lot in life and the great trial he was going through. Then God called him to account and asked:

> *Where were you when I laid the foundation of the earth? Tell Me, if you have understanding, who set its measurements?* **Since you know.** *Or who stretched the line on it? On what were its bases sunk? Or who laid its cornerstone, when the morning stars sang together and* **all the sons of God shouted for joy** (Job 38:4-7).

Then God continues:

> *Surely you know, for you were already born! You have lived so many years* (Job 38:21 NIV).

> *But of course you know all this! For you were born before it was all created, and you are so very experienced* (Job 38:21 NLT).

You were there when God created the world.

This Scripture makes it clear that Job was one of the sons of God who shouted for joy when this world was created. You were there when God created the world. We don't recall or remember because the details are lost—they fade and are veiled when we enter this life on earth and become clothed in mortal flesh.

Your spirit is very old and knows much more than what your mind has comprehended so far. When your heart and mind agree, all things are possible to you in Christ Jesus. Ask. Knock. Seek. Search for the truth and let it set you free.

Question to Ponder

Why do you think it is important that we understand that our spirit was born long before we were born on earth?

_____

_____

_____

_____

_____

The Spirit of Man

Your spirit is the real you. God is breaking the outer person so that you can live from your spirit and not your soul. Many Christians' spirits are encased within the soul, trapped by the physical body, and beaten down by appetites of the flesh. God is cracking the outer core so the Spirit will beam forth from our spirit.

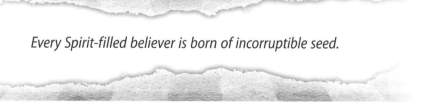

Every Spirit-filled believer is born of incorruptible seed.

God put His own genetic code in your spirit. His "seed" abides in you, encased in your spirit. You are born not of a corruptible seed but an incorruptible seed by the Word of God, which lives and abides inside of you. Every Spirit-filled believer is born of incorruptible seed (see 1 John 3:9). However, even though God put His very own nature into our spirit, most of us live out of the soul. This is important to lay hold of—it is already placed within you, but everything emerges through faith. Faith, though, comes by understanding, and understanding is vital to the maturation process.

The Seed of God

Maturation happens when Christ grows to maturity from the seed God planted in your spirit until you are fully formed in the image and the likeness of Him. Your personality does not change, but your spirit becomes a perfect "clone" of the Lord Jesus Christ living in and through you. You do not have to fast and seek God for these characteristics or for His nature—all of it is already in you by reason of the new birth.

The Church today has been in a place of stunted growth for too long. When you are born again, all of God's nature was placed into your spirit. All we have to do is release and acknowledge Christ in us because His DNA and characteristics in us cannot sin or fail. His DNA in us is pure, faultless, sinless, and unfailing. Thus, the one born of God does not sin.

You can sin with your soul, but that holy DNA in your spirit—the DNA born of God—cannot sin. This is why there is a battle between the soul and spirit. Ultimately, God wants the inner person to emerge victorious.

Question to Ponder

As far as spiritual growth is concerned, some people simply don't grow or mature at all while others mature rapidly. Why do you think this is true?

_____

_____

_____

_____

_____

_____

Complete in Him

You are complete in Him—you do not need any more than that. All the treasures of wisdom and knowledge are in Him, and all of Him is in that divine seed that has been planted in each of us (see Col. 2:3). This is why the apostle Paul said that we have the mind of Christ (see 1 Cor. 2:16).

And in Him you have been made complete, and He is the head over all rule and authority (Colossians 2:10).

It is not about having more of the mind of Christ but tapping into the fullness of what is already programmed in there—all wisdom and knowledge. All of who God is resides in your spirit. You are complete in Him. In Him dwells the fullness of the godhead; this is also in you. When you get this, when the Body of Christ gets this truth and lays hold of it, the Church as we know it will be transformed into a mature Bride. God wants to bring forth sons and daughters of God who have the fullness and completeness of God flowing from them (see 1 John 4:4; John 16:13).

The real you is not an insignificant person, for you are made in the image and likeness of God. This whole world awaits a manifestation, a coming forth, a revealing of people who will walk in the image and the likeness of God. This requires putting the soul life to death and placing your will, thoughts, emotions, and desires into subjection to your spirit (see 1 John 2:27; 2 Cor. 5:17).

You are a new creation in Christ!

Questions to Ponder

Why are we already complete in Christ? What does this knowledge do to your confidence to pursue spiritual things?

_____

_____

_____

_____

_____

You Are "gods"?

Jesus answered them, "Has it not been written in your Law 'I said, you are gods'?" (John 10:34).

This was not a question of Christ classifying people as deity but as the offspring of deity. We are the spiritual sons and daughters of God the Father, partakers of His divine nature, and appointed as His representatives to rule and govern in the kingdom territory called earth. Jesus was not saying that we would be gods in our own right or added to the godhead in any way. Our mandate is and always has been to come to be like God (see 1 John 3:2).

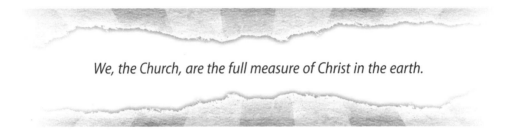

We, the Church, are the full measure of Christ in the earth.

God called His newly created, formed, and framed firstborn son "very good." When the Father breathed into Adam's nostrils the breath of life, all of the DNA of the Creator was deposited into him body, soul, and spirit. He was God's offspring, a son of His love, fruit of His own nature, created in His image.

We, the Church, are the full measure of Christ in the earth, complete in Him, bone of His bone, and flesh of His flesh (see Eph. 1:22-23). We are the image of God, and having the revelation of this alive inside of us is the beginning of complete and total victory. We must understand who we are in Him.

The Creation Law of Reproduction

God's design was that everything created would "bring forth" after its own kind (see Gen. 1:11-12). Birds are birds; they bring forth birds after their likeness. An apple tree brings forth apples. God brought forth a son after His own kind, a family member who was formed, fashioned, and equipped with His DNA to look like Him and act like Him, even creating and co-creating with Him in the earth! God walked and talked with Adam in the cool of the day in relationship. Adam was completely natural and supernatural, spiritual and physical. *"Then the Lord God took the man and put him into the garden of Eden to cultivate it and keep it"* (Gen. 2:15).

Adam accomplished his God-appointed tasks by supernatural ability. He was an authoritative son of Glory moving without restraint in the earth. By subduing knowledge, wisdom, and understanding, all Adam had to do was think of what needed to be accomplished, and as he spoke it was created. All he needed to do was simply speak of the place he needed to be and he was there and the task was completed just as he imagined it. Adam moved back and forth on the earth in the spiritual dimension, as quickly as a thought, just as the angels of God did.

Adam acted as a literal son of the Most High God. He was fully engaged in spirit, soul, and body at all times and his connection or fellowship with Heaven was never broken.

QUESTIONS FOR GROUP DISCUSSION

If we are truly complete in Christ, why do you think we work so hard at becoming like Him? We're not called to *work toward* attaining completeness, but *work from* being complete in Christ—from our new nature, our new man, our new identity. Why do you think people still struggle with an unhealthy "works" mentality?

_____

_____

_____

_____

_____

_____

_____

In what ways is it easy for you to understand how you are made in the image of God? Are there some aspects of God's nature that are difficult for you to totally embrace that you are made in that same likeness? If so, why is it hard to believe this about yourself?

_____

_____

_____

_____

_____

_____

_____

_____

LIFE APPLICATION

You, too, were sent from the presence of God to this earth to fulfill a high and noble calling. This world is not your home. You are here on a mission. Your mission is to bring Heaven to earth. It is God's purpose that you someday will return home a much greater, nobler spirit in the image and likeness of Jesus Christ. Meditate on these things and let these biblical truths fill you with awe.

_____

_____

_____

_____

_____

_____

_____

_____

_____

_____

_____

_____

_____

_____

_____

_____

GLORY RISING

Chapter 12

THE POWER OF THE TRANSFORMED MIND

Satan is very much aware of the power of the transformed mind and constantly assaults our minds, which are his greatest battlefields. Whoever wins the battle for our minds is whose servants we'll become. Paul commanded us to think on virtuous things. We cannot allow our minds to dwell upon evil or things that are incompatible with God and expect to be compatible with Him.

Do not be deceived: "Evil company corrupts good habits"
(1 Corinthians 15:33 NKJV).

We have within us the ability to renew our minds and be transformed. The mind is malleable. Humankind has a creative capacity. We operate in that capacity either consciously or unconsciously. Thoughts are seeds. When thoughts are connected with strong emotion, they become seeds and conception takes place. If that seed is nurtured and incubated, it will reproduce according to the particular framework of that particular pattern of thought, whether for evil or for good. Seed thoughts will manifest and come to pass! One of the most important laws of the Kingdom is that all things reproduce after their own likeness and kind. Your thoughts will reproduce after their own kind.

Questions to Ponder

What do you think it means to operate in a creative capacity consciously? What does it mean to operate in a creative capacity unconsciously?

_____

_____

_____

_____

The Programmable Mind

The minds of people are difficult to understand. The human brain is an incredible bioelectric, magnetic mass of gray matter and works similar to a computer. The mind is programmable. It can be programmed with ideas, concepts, knowledge, and values and will run according to its programming. Satan wants to program your mind to run according to his program with lies and values that are contrary to God's thoughts and ways.

The good news is that God sent us an instruction manual (the Bible) that explains the marvel of the mind and how to use it. It reveals valuable keys to the right and proper use of the mind. It explains why we're incapable, in and of ourselves, of working out His purpose without His divine intervention.

Question to Ponder

Can you give some examples of how the Bible talks about the proper use of the mind?

_____

_____

_____

_____

_____

A Receptor and Gateway

When thoughts and emotions blend, a creative process of birthing starts in the thought life and in the realm of the imagination. Satan knows this, so the battle is for who controls your mind. The mind is the gateway and connector to all incoming spiritual communication.

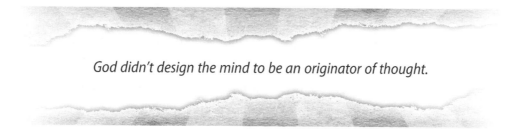

God didn't design the mind to be an originator of thought.

The physical brain is different from the mind. The brain is the physical housing and connector used by the mind to translate spiritually inspired information communicated from the realm of the spirit. The brain then transfers this information into the natural. Bill Johnson states, "God didn't design the mind to be an originator of thought." Rather, He designed the mind to act as an internal processor capable of receiving programmable information—information that could be programmed into the "system."[1]

Whoever programs your mind will determine the way you think and how your life evolves—what your life will become or your destiny.

Question to Ponder

Describe the difference between the physical brain and the mind as you understand it. What capacity does each have to serve the Kingdom of God?

_____

_____

_____

_____

_____

_____

Acquiring Knowledge

We gain spiritual knowledge by developing and using our spiritual senses. When we draw close to God and allow God to strengthen, teach, and lead us through and by His Spirit, spiritual desires spring forth and we accomplish spiritual things. With a Spirit-led mind, we will find the way into that supernatural realm of God's Kingdom and all of its treasures.

Sometimes we end up with wrong programming that runs contrary to the design of God; however, when we are born again, we are supernaturally infused with the holy seed of God. In that very seed is *all* of who God is. In time, with the proper care from the Holy Spirit and the Word, that seed will grow and bear the exact likeness and makeup of the original Seed. Contained in the seed is all of who God is spiritually and the very likeness and image of Christ Jesus.

Question to Ponder

If we can spiritually see God's Kingdom, how much more will we desire it?

_____

_____

_____

_____

_____

When Mind and Spirit Agree

When you examine an acorn, it seems impossible that a huge tree is in that seed, but it is. Given the right climate and soil conditions, it will naturally become a huge tree. So too, with the Seed of God planted in you, given the right conditions, you'll grow to become like Him. Planted in you is the very mind of Christ. Deep within your spirit—which is joined to the Holy Spirit—is the mind of Christ Jesus. He who is joined to the Lord is one spirit (see Phil. 1:27).

Planted in you is the very mind of Christ.

Reprogramming Your Mind

Light will flow into your being and the transformation process will begin when there's harmony between your mind and your spirit. Harmony comes through freedom from blockages, renewal, and reprogramming of the mind.

Your mind is the gateway between the spirit and physical realm for the whole person, so your mind and spirit must agree. When you were born again your spirit and mind were no longer compatible, so it's an ongoing process to reprogram the mind to conform to the mind of Christ in your spirit (see Eph. 4:23).

Your mind can originate thought as part of the creative process. However, it can also be *inspired* by your spirit and the Holy Spirit within you. The spiritual person must be programmed with different thinking (see 1 Cor. 2:14; 2:12; 6:17).

Questions to Ponder

How does your mind operate as a gateway between the spirit and the physical realm? Why must they agree?

_____

_____

_____

_____

_____

The First Step to Renewal

Your brain has to be transformed from the soulish concepts of the world by the Word of God, which you receive whether you understand it or not (see Rom. 12:2). The greatest hindrance to walking with God is the unrenewed brain.

If we can get our thinking patterns renewed to be compatible with our spirit man, there will be a unity that will allow light, understanding, and knowledge to flow into our being and transform us. We will understand God and the purposes of God because our brains will be in harmony with Him. The supernatural pathways only open when the two become compatible.

Questions to Ponder

Have you thought that your brain was in harmony with God in a certain activity or understanding? How did you know this to be true?

_____

_____

_____

_____

_____

An Ancient Spirit

Your spirit came from Heaven and has been in existence for a long time. I am talking spirit here, not soul. The soul can die. God can take the soul, or the soul can be forfeited by a person. The soul can also be saved and redeemed (see Ps. 86:13; 116:4; 2 Sam. 4:9). Therefore, the soul is what each person is as a human being. A person cannot exist outside of the soul. The Old Testament reveals nothing about any pre-existence or immortality of the soul.

It was God's intention that we grow beyond just spirit and become a new creation.

But the spirit is another matter. It pre-existed in Heaven; however, it is clothed in the soul. Your spirit came into your body at birth. It was God's intention that we grow beyond just spirit and become a new creation (see 1 Thess. 5:23). It is important that we as spirit, soul, and body blend as one so we can interact with the spiritual realm and the physical realm.

Start Now

Our dreams and vision must be in line with what God has called us to and what our future is. If we can start to get even a small amount of compatibility between our spirit and our brain, we will start to fill up with light. We will see the wonders of God. We will begin to understand like never before. The creative side of our life will begin to blossom, and we will begin to flow into our destiny.

God will have a supernatural people, a Glory generation, in these last days doing great things we never thought possible. We have to be changed now—we have to become the overcoming Body of Christ—if we with Christ will rule the world. We have to align our minds and spirits if we're to do the "all things are possible." We can have such an impact on the Glory harvest when we enlarge our thinking by aligning it with our spirit. Going to church every Sunday will not do it, but having Heaven's mind will.

Questions to Ponder

Why must your dreams and visions align with God's purpose and destiny for you? What does the agreement between what you see and God's will open up in terms of possibilities for your life?

_____

_____

_____

_____

_____

_____

Take Back Your Mind

The battlefield is in the mind. We have a fierce adversary who wants control of it. How do we take it back? By the casting down of imaginations and of every high thing that exalts itself against the knowledge of God. Thus, we are to bring every thought into captivity and into the obedience of Christ (see 2 Cor. 10:5).

Spiritual gates open wide to the spiritual sons and daughters of God who will find access into Eden's door and to the Tree of Life. They are destiny's double doors that will open for you to encounter God in genuine, tangible ways, executing and partaking of the ever-increasing and all-powerful realm of Glory in the Kingdom of God for His Glory. Are you ready to break into new dimensions of the realities of the Glory realm of God?

Endnote

1. Bill Johnson, *The Supernatural Power of the Renewed Mind,* audio teaching (Redding, CA: Bethel Church).

QUESTIONS FOR GROUP DISCUSSION

How have you reprogrammed your mind in specific aspects of your life to conform to Christ's model?

_____

_____

_____

_____

_____

_____

_____

_____

Paul told the Romans that the natural mind is an enemy of God (see Rom. 8:7). Your spirit may be born again, but if your mind is unrenewed, there is conflict. Why is this true?

_____

_____

_____

_____

_____

_____

_____

_____

LIFE APPLICATION

…whatever is true, whatever is worthy of reverence and is honorable and seemly, whatever is just, whatever is pure, whatever is lovely and lovable, whatever is kind and winsome and gracious, if there is any virtue and excellence, if there is anything worthy of praise, think on and weigh and take account of these things [fix your minds on them] (Philippians 4:8 AMP).

How can you use this to guard your mind at all times? How can it act as a filter that you place over your mind?

_____

_____

_____

_____

_____

_____

_____

_____

_____

_____

_____

_____

_____

_____

_____

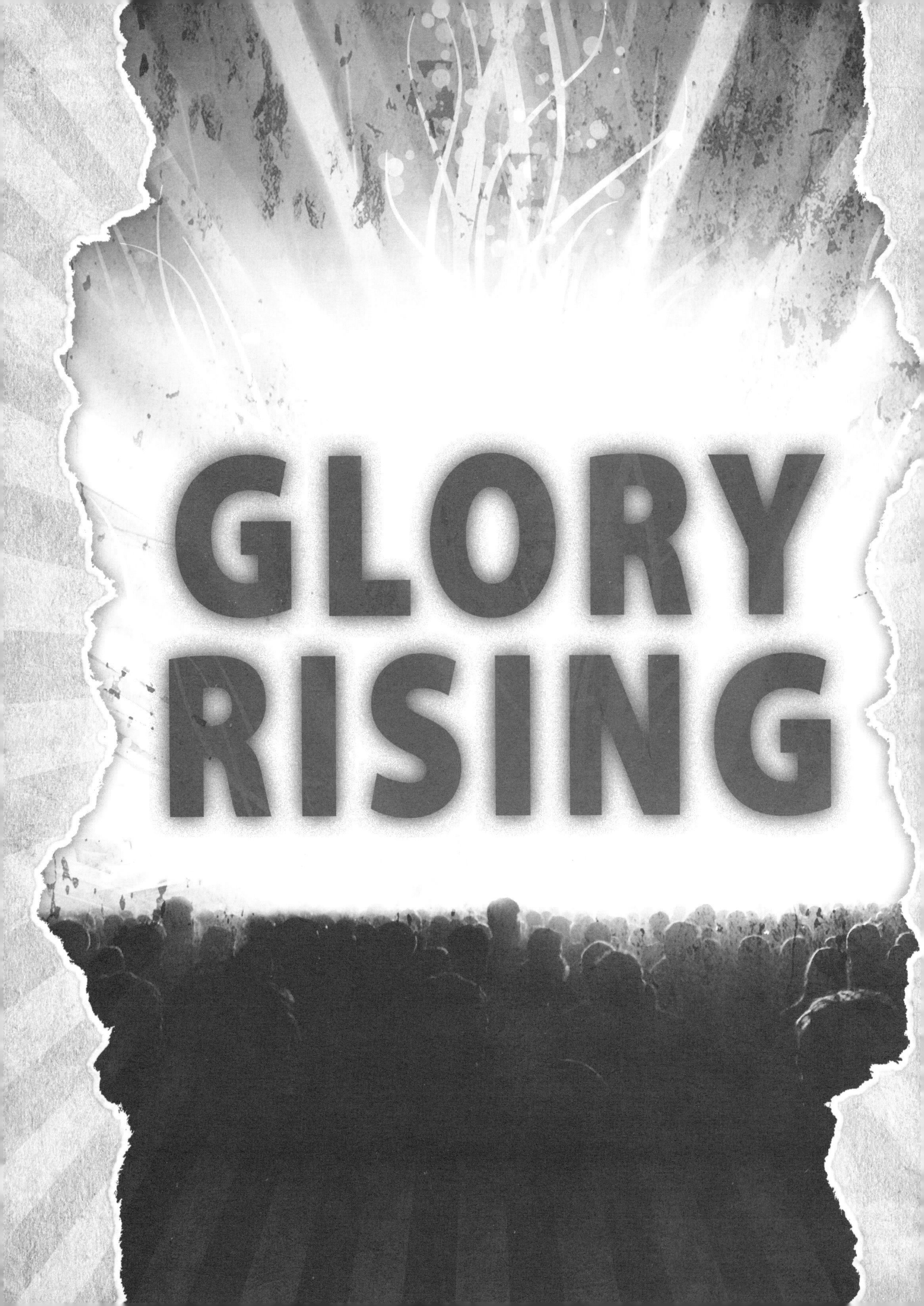
GLORY
RISING

Chapter 13

THE CREATIVE POWER OF THOUGHTS

And do not be conformed to this world, but be transformed by the renewing of your mind, so that you may prove what the will of God is, that which is good and acceptable and perfect (Romans 12:2).

aul is exhorting the believers in Rome not to conform to the world with its traditions and ways of thinking. He is saying that our entire lives will be transformed and metamorphosed when our minds are renewed.

A *mind-set* is when our minds are programmed and set to respond a specific way or project a certain impression when encountering different words, pictures, situations, etc. Ungodly and worldly mind-sets are spiritual strongholds that restrain us from soaring. We are liberated through the constrictions and pressures that the Lord allows to come upon us. The restraints of self-dependence are broken as we rely more and more on the Spirit of God, being strengthened in our inner person so we can rise to higher altitudes.

Question to Ponder

How have you seen God work on your worldly mind-sets using constrictions and pressures?

_____

_____

_____

_____

_____

_____

_____

Thoughts Birthed From Passion

Thoughts are simply seeds. Passion and strong desire are the heat that causes the seed to spin into life. Babies are conceived in passion. So too, inner passion gives life to the seeds in our heart.

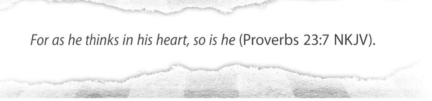

For as he thinks in his heart, so is he (Proverbs 23:7 NKJV).

This means that as a person believes and thinks in his heart, so he will become. When your emotions agree with your thinking, it shall be done! (See Mark 11:25; Matt. 18:19.) The power and Glory of God in the anointing are released through the gateway of human affection. When our thinking connects with our feelings, a seed is planted by desire and a power is released (see James 1:15).

We must visualize what we desire to become in God. Actually, we must see ourselves as we really are in Christ; then it will manifest as reality in our lives. The imagination is a creative tool that brings into the physical world that which sits dormant in the unseen realm. We can use our imagination to transform the world around us, both for good and for evil.

Creation Responds to Love

All of creation was preprogrammed to respond to love. If we have love emanating out from us, the smallest atom can feel it and will respond to it. Atoms were birthed from love, and as created particles they feel love and respond to it. Atoms will cooperate with what you desire and speak because they recognize your sonship and know that you have dominion over the world (see Rom. 8:19,21).

When the complete and perfect comes (love), the incomplete and imperfect will vanish away (see 1 Cor. 13:10). All creation responds to the more excellent and perfect way of love. Signs, wonders, and miracles come through love; we have to keep unbelief out.

Doubt opens the door to unbelief, and unbelief is a tremendously evil power that cuts us off from the promises of God (see James 1:7-8). We must deal violently with this spirit. We shouldn't have even a speck of doubt in our hearts.

Questions to Ponder

Have you ever thought about atoms responding to love before reading this? What does this principle of love mean for your daily life?

_____

_____

_____

_____

Unity of Spirit, Soul, and Body

The reality is we are spirit, but God gave us a soul and body also. We are new creations in Christ (see 2 Cor. 5:17). Yes, we are spirit beings, but we are human beings too. All of our spirit, soul, and body need to come into alignment with the Kingdom of God—this only happens through the spirit first, though.

Now may the God of peace Himself sanctify you entirely; and may your spirit and soul and body be preserved complete... (1 Thessalonians 5:23).

It is important that spirit, soul, and body blend as one so we can interact with the spiritual realm and the physical realm. When you were born again, Christ came into your spirit, and in that seed is the fullness of the godhead: Father, Son, and Holy Spirit. You are filled with eternity past, present, and future. *"But you have an anointing from the Holy One, and you know all things"* (1 John 2:20 NKJV).

Let It Be Done

Everything God spoke into existence already existed in His mind and in His heart. Everything that a person builds first lives within him or her—within the imagination.

We know that faith is not just a matter of the mind but also of the heart. As we fix our gaze on Jesus and keep seeking the things above (see Col. 3:1-2) with our minds and imaginations, we will get breakthrough; we will literally get to see the eternal realm. We must learn to take every thought captive to the obedience of Christ and set our affections on things above (see 2 Cor. 10:5). We will start to see ourselves and everyone around us through the eyes of Christ. We will start to *see* our destiny and our future Glory. Then, and only then, will we be able to pull it into today.

Question to Ponder

Explain how your faith is a matter of your heart. How is your faith connected to your mind?

_____

_____

_____

_____

_____

Language of Vision

*Since we consider and **look** not to the things that are seen but to the things that are **unseen;** for the things that are visible are temporal (brief and fleeting), but **the things that are invisible are deathless and everlasting** (2 Corinthians 4:18 AMP).*

We do this by looking with the eyes of our heart—with the eyes of our imagination. When we look with the eyes of understanding, we are gazing into the eternal realm—the real realm.

God can speak to us through the imagination, the devil can speak to us through the imagination, and we can use our own imagination. Train your mind and exercise your spiritual senses to discern the voice of God from among all the other voices (see Heb. 5:14). If you want to walk with God, you will have to learn to walk with Him in your imagination, having the eyes of your understanding enlightened that you may know the things of God.

Question to Ponder

What do you think is involved in training your mind and exercising your spiritual senses to discern the voice of God from any other voice?

_____

_____

_____

_____

The Key for Creativity

The imagination is our gift from God that should be used as a tool to create and manifest the unseen into the seen. God has created us to be a thinking, imaginative, and visionary people who, with the sanctified imagination, like God, *"…calls into being that which does not exist"* (Rom. 4:17). God has given us the power to create, and not just through procreation or reproduction but in many different ways, including artistically and visually.

We are inventive and creative like our Father in Heaven.

Every physical item that surrounds you right now, whether it's a clock, a picture frame, or a coffee cup, has a certain amount of imagination and creative design put into it. Every masterpiece ever created first existed in the imagination of the artist.

Question to Ponder

What do you think is the difference between using your imagination as a tool for God's handiwork and vain imaginations?

_____

_____

_____

_____

_____

_____

_____

_____

What's Your Vision?

It is important that we see ourselves the way God sees us. We are citizens of Heaven. We must be transformed from natural ways of thinking to heavenly ways. In Genesis 2:7, God breathed the breath of life into Adam, and he became the first living *soul*. When God breathed the breath of life, He breathed all eternity into Adam—Adam's destiny, identity, citizenship, origin, imagination, and the Spirit of Wisdom and Understanding all came out of the eternity of eternities, directly out of God, and into Adam.

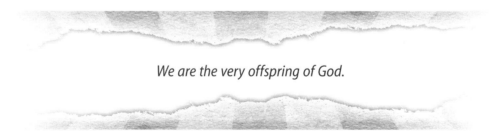

We are the very offspring of God.

We are citizens of Heaven; our origin is not from here. We can use our imaginations to creatively bring into the natural that which exists in the spirit. We can release the will of God for our families, friends, ministries, businesses, cities, states, and the nations.

Question to Ponder

What is your vision for the release of God's will through you?

_____

_____

_____

_____

_____

_____

_____

_____

_____

Sealed and Ordered

You have a blueprint and destiny from God within your spirit that's unchangeable. Most often the desires in our hearts are the very things God has *sealed* and *ordered* in us by the Holy Spirit. We are capable of bringing out and birthing our destinies. If we don't, we will agonize over it until it happens. Many of us wonder what the will of God is for our lives when it's already written all over us.

Unless we exercise our imaginations in a sanctified manner as God intended and take back the right to use our imaginations from the devil, we will be at a great disadvantage. God loves dreamers and visionaries who believe His Word. We need to get hold of God and let Him get hold of us. We need to shake Heaven until we see the full fruit of our hearts' desires come to pass.

QUESTIONS FOR GROUP DISCUSSION

What are some of your positive heavenly mind-sets? What are some of your ungodly, worldly mind-sets you are trying to change?

_____

_____

_____

_____

_____

_____

_____

_____

If what you think and believe in your heart about yourself is what you will become, what do you think in your heart about yourself right now?

_____

_____

_____

_____

_____

_____

_____

_____

_____

LIFE APPLICATION

Take some time to meditate before God and ask Him to show you how He sees you. He sees the completed you—the you that exists in eternity—the finished product. You might be blown away with how He sees you! It may not look like the present you at all. When you glimpse yourself through Christ's eyes, choose to align yourself with the you who exists in the eternal realm. This actually brings your future self and destiny into the realm of now. Ask the Lord what *spiritual* and *practical* steps need to be taken to help you move forward in the renewal and transformation of your life and mind.

_____

_____

_____

_____

_____

_____

_____

_____

_____

_____

_____

_____

_____

_____

_____

_____

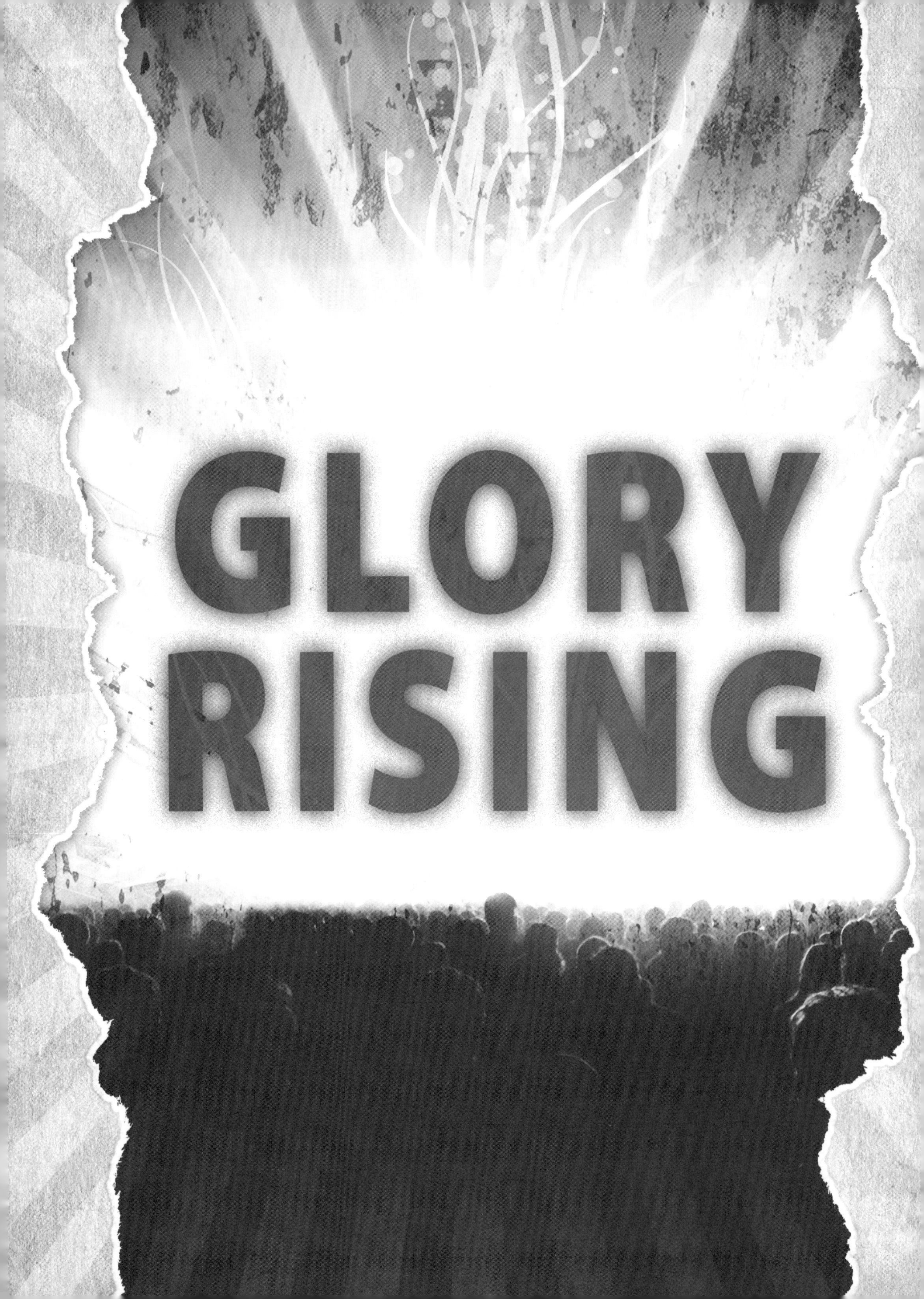
GLORY
RISING

Chapter 14

GLORY ATMOSPHERES

One of the glorious mysteries of the Kingdom is the existence of supernatural gates, windows, passageways, and doors. These are portals leading to and from the heavens where angels can come and go, moving up and down in the realm of Glory. When you're standing in a Glory portal, there is an open Heaven around you. A Glory portal is a "spherical opening of light" reaching between Heaven and earth, offering divine protection by which "angels and heavenly beings" can come and go without demonic interference.

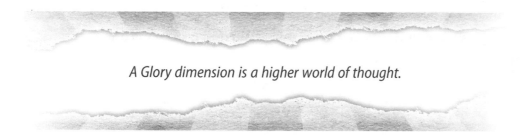

A Glory dimension is a higher world of thought.

Heavenly beings and the angels of God flow through spherical Glory portals as streams of love and light bringing revelation, power, strength, and healing virtue to the believer. These portals of Glory, or Glory dimensions, exist as supernatural pathways, doors, spheres, levels, or stages that unlock the process of revelation and its mysteries that are revealed and opened up to the believer by understanding. A Glory dimension is a higher world of thought. Glory dimensions are not far from us but are right in front of us at all times. By understanding and decree, they open up as heavenly gates and establish Kingdom realities that manifest substance in our midst. Understanding alone won't open them; we need to be speaking in faith what we see. Paul called them the heavenly realm (see Eph. 1:3; 2:6).

Question to Ponder

"Glory dimensions are not far from us, but are right in front of us at all times." Have you found this to be true in your experience?

_____

_____

_____

_____

_____

_____

_____

Heaven Around Us

Heaven is around us at all times, and when connected like a radio frequency, it pulls that heavenly dimension into the natural and manifests it. The word spoken in faith brings a creative activation of substance in the realm of the spirit, resulting in manifested miracles, healings, signs, and wonders.

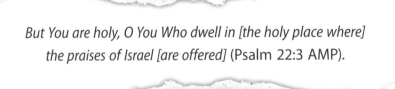

But You are holy, O You Who dwell in [the holy place where]
the praises of Israel [are offered] (Psalm 22:3 AMP).

Jesus is *enthroned* upon the praises of His people. Jehoshaphat, king of Judah, led the people into battle against the Moabites and men of Ammon and Mount Seir that were without number. The singers and the priests were in front, leading the way into battle singing (see 2 Chron. 20:22). The atmosphere of praise and thanksgiving completely destroyed the works of the devil.

Questions to Ponder

Have you ever seen the atmosphere change when you praised and gave thanks to God?

_____

_____

_____

_____

_____

What are some examples you remember from Scripture that show how praise and thanksgiving make a difference in receiving breakthroughs, miracles, and healings?

_____

_____

_____

_____

_____

Establishing Atmosphere

Bismark Tudor tells us:

Atmosphere is created as the result of spiritual influence and pull whether good and bad. Once the spiritual influence is established that atmosphere when maintained over a prolonged period of time will create a spiritual climate.[1]

God is calling us in this season to change the atmosphere into a spiritual climate.

When climates are sustained and maintained, whether good or bad, over a prolonged period of time, they create strongholds. Strongholds in turn bring about the belief systems that establish behavior in a society.

It is these belief systems that create behavior. Satan is the master of atmosphere. He is the prince of the power of the air in Ephesians 2:2. We are all continually being influenced by atmosphere, whether good or bad.

We change the atmosphere by speaking and releasing the prophetic decree into an atmosphere of Glory. Our words are powerful. When spoken in faith and full belief of the final outcome, our words contain the framework and creative power of Spirit and life to birth things in the physical. Jesus said the words He speaks are Spirit and Life (see John 6:63). If a climate can be created, that means it can be sustained if conditions are maintained. Climates are prevalent at every level in society.

Question to Ponder

How can we change the atmosphere around us by speaking and releasing prophetic decrees into an atmosphere of Glory?

_____

_____

_____

_____

_____

The Spoken Decree

We as believers have the ability to speak into the Glory and bring an atmosphere that changes the spiritual climate by the spirit of faith. The release of that spoken decree will open the spirit world and bring the Glory of God that will change the atmospheric condition (see John 22:28).

Glory comes when faith is released. It is then when we can call things that are not as though they are by prophetic decree and they are created. Destinies are released, body parts are created and re-created, sickness is destroyed, finances are brought forth, ministries are birthed, and signs and wonders are performed that confirm the word. If the devil tells you that your body is riddled with sickness, don't agree with him. If he tells you that you are bankrupt, don't agree with him. Respond with the prophetic decree that by His stripes we are and were healed. We are the rich and not poor—the head and not the tail (see Deut. 28).

If we can agree with God touching any one thing on the earth, it can be birthed out of the realm of Glory. When we start creating with our words, the devil is in trouble. His world will crumble and cannot recover. We are then reclaiming and re-creating the atmosphere and reclaiming what was lost in Eden.

Question to Ponder

How do we know if we have come into agreement with God?

_____

_____

_____

_____

_____

Sustaining the Glory

Glory portals open up in the throne room, travel through the second heaven, and open up on Earth. Glory portals open when drawn upon by faith. When faith pulls, then Heaven manifests at that place of our belief. Our job is to have faith and create spiritual hunger to establish an atmosphere for the Glory of God that will pull substance into the natural.

Getting the Glory to come is one thing, but creating an environment that will sustain the Glory is another. We can have powerful explosions of the Glory of God with miracles, but if we don't sustain that atmosphere of Glory in revival, we cannot change our churches, cities, states, regions, and nations. All authority has been given to Jesus in earth and Heaven (see Matt. 28:18). When we wake up and understand that we've been given all authority as the Body of Christ, we will then be able to take back control over the spiritual conditions of entire cities, regions, and nations. The world has been longing to see a people who not only claim to know God, but also walk, talk, and act like Him.

It is God's desire that the glorious light and power of His presence would shine in and through a Glory generation of believers all across the globe (see 2 Cor. 4:6). But in order for us to bring Heaven to earth, we must first bring earth to Heaven (see Exod. 20:12; Ps. 25:4). Throughout Scripture, we see the existence of doorways or Glory portals (see Ps. 24:7; Prov. 8:34; John 1:51).

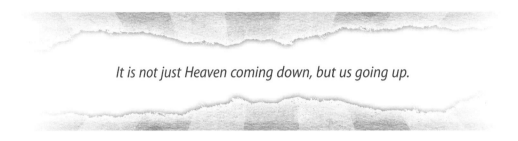

It is not just Heaven coming down, but us going up.

After these things I looked, and behold, a door standing open in heaven. And the first voice which I heard was like a trumpet speaking with me, saying "Come up here, and I will show you things which must take place after this." Immediately I was in the Spirit… (Revelation 4:1-2 NKJV).

The "door" in Revelation suggests God's invitation for us to come up to His heavenly realm. As His friends, the Lord wants to open the portals of Heaven and release an unparalleled visitation of heavenly hosts. It is not just Heaven coming down, but us going up.

Question to Ponder

How should the fact that Matthew 28:18 tells us that all authority has been given to Jesus in earth and Heaven affect your faith and prayer life?

_____

_____

_____

_____

_____

_____

_____

Jacob Finds a Door

Jacob spent the night in a place where his forefather Abraham had called upon the name of the Lord (see Gen. 28:16-17). As he rested his head upon a covenant stone, a portal, or a heavenly door, opened. Jacob saw a vision of a ladder with angels ascending and descending on it. When he awoke from sleep, he said:

> ...Surely the Lord is in this place, and I did not know it. ...How awesome is this place! This is none other than the house of God, and this is the gate of heaven (Genesis 28:16-17 NKJV).

Jacob marked the stairway to Heaven and named the place "Bethel," or "dwelling place of God." Several times after this, the Lord told Jacob to return to Bethel where He would speak to him further. Have you ever wondered why the Lord, who could speak to a person anywhere, would instruct Jacob to go back to Bethel so He could speak with him further? Bethel was a literal portal. This is the same place the Lord led Abraham to sacrifice Isaac. It is a designated place by God for communication between Heaven and earth. God told Elijah to eat angel cake that would give him strength to get him to the portal of Mount Horeb. While God was talking to Elijah, He instructed the prophet to go to Mount Horeb, also known as Mount Sinai, where the Lord would talk to him further (see 1 Kings 19:5-8).

Divine portals into the heavenly realm exist around the earth today. The city of Jerusalem is a portal. In fact, it is the major portal on the face of the earth. That's why both David and Isaiah said that Jerusalem is the center of the earth. The occult and the kingdom of darkness understand the reality of dark portals in the spirit as well and guard them with great fervor. I've been told of great battles that church leaders in the United States, who actually purchased property to build their churches on, have gone through. Many of them had to fight for existence, as it seemed all hell had come against them.

God is calling His people to take back these high places so that His angels can come and go without hindrance. Begin to take authority and establish the atmosphere of Heaven everywhere your feet tread. You have power to dictate and decree a thing so it will be established. Start decreeing daily to create Glory atmospheres everywhere you go.

Endnote

1.   Tudor Bismark, *Dimensions, Atmospheres, and Climates*, audio teaching (www.jabula.org).

QUESTIONS FOR GROUP DISCUSSION

How can we create the faith and spiritual hunger necessary to establish an atmosphere for the Glory of God to pull substance into the natural realm?

_____

_____

_____

_____

_____

_____

_____

As stated in this chapter, "The world has been longing to see a people who not only claim to know God, but walk, talk, and act like Him...." In what ways do you feel God calling you to portray His character, nature, and power in the earth?

_____

_____

_____

_____

_____

_____

_____

_____

LIFE APPLICATION

Jeff Jansen encourages us to "take authority…[and] start decreeing daily to create Glory atmospheres everywhere you go." Where is your targeted area on the earth for establishing the atmosphere and dominion of Heaven?

_____

_____

_____

_____

_____

_____

_____

_____

_____

_____

_____

_____

_____

_____

_____

_____

_____

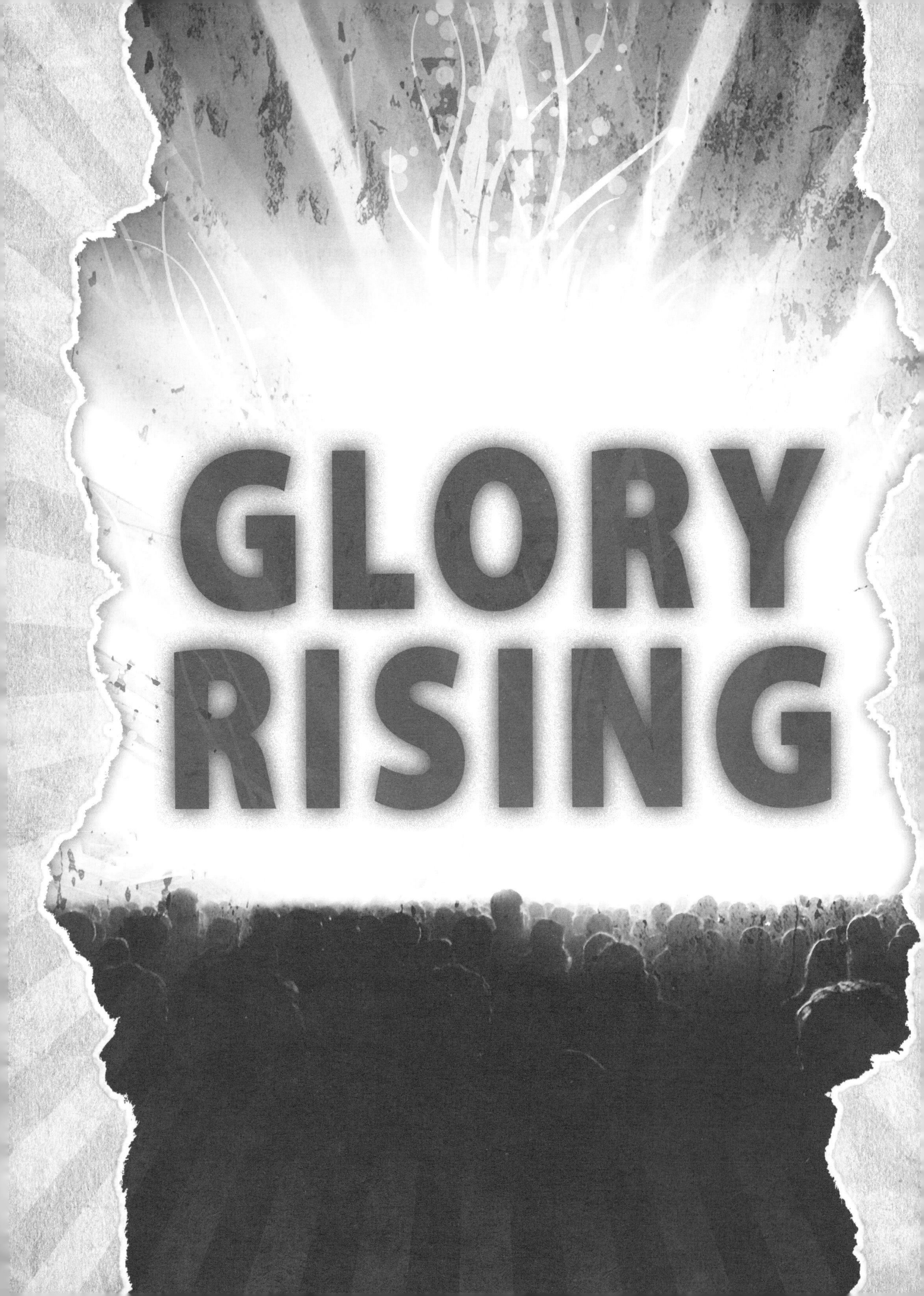
GLORY
RISING

REDISCOVERING THE ANCIENT PATHWAYS

This is what the Lord says: "Stand at the crossroads and look; ask for the ancient paths, ask where the good way is, and walk in it, and you will find rest for your souls…" (Jeremiah 6:16 NIV).

Jesus walked the ancient pathways with God and chose to follow them even unto death, opening up for us a new and living way that leads us back home to the Father. Jesus opened up the "Way" through the veil of His flesh. He offered Himself willingly to bring us back to God. In order to get back to Eden, we need to walk the way Jesus walked. His was a life of contemplation, prayer, devotion, and communion with the Father.

Jesus opened the ancient pathway to us by offering Himself as a living sacrifice to God. He Himself said, *"I am the way"* (John 14:6). The way back to what? The way back to Eden—for through a man, death came to all of humankind. So by one Man all are made alive (see 1 Cor. 15:21-22).

Adam had borne the image of God and was created from the dust of the earth. He enjoyed blissful friendship with the Lord, walking and talking daily with Him as a father would enjoy his son. Our relationship to God was cut off, but Jesus, the "heavenly Man," opened up the ancient roads once again as One who bears the image of a heavenly Man. Jesus became a "Life-Giving Spirit" and restored humankind to the place from which we fell (see 1 Cor. 15:45-49).

Questions to Ponder

What is your understanding of how Christ opened up ancient pathways for you? What are these pathways as you discern them?

_____

_____

_____

_____

_____

_____

Enoch Walked the Ancient Pathways

Enoch walked with God on the ancient pathways and was no more, for God took him (see Gen. 5:22-24). Enoch spent so much time on these supernatural highways that God finally kept him. Enoch walked in the heavenlies with the Lord and knew the vast resources of that place with all its limitless dimensions in the spirit realm. He was even asked to make amends between the fallen angels and the Creator.[1]

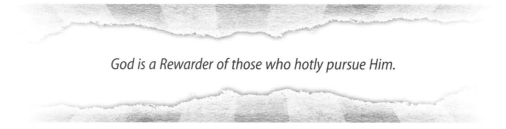

God is a Rewarder of those who hotly pursue Him.

With the help of the angels, God granted Enoch access into His presence. He moved on the ancient pathways originally designed for humankind. His relentless quest to know God opened the heavens that were shut off to most. God is a Rewarder of those who hotly pursue Him. Enoch wrote down many of his revelations and encounters in the heavenly realms. They are recorded in the "Book of Enoch." It was quite clear that the early church had and quoted the Book of Enoch and highly valued it. Jesus, Peter, and Jude all cited passages from it. Even though it is not considered Canon, it is like other documented chronicles detailing Enoch's travels to Heaven and his communications with the Lord.

Question to Ponder

Do you have a "relentless quest" to know God? Determine the reason for your answer.

_____

_____

_____

_____

_____

_____

_____

The Heart of God

From the beginning of time, God has always longed for a people who would be completely His—a family in the earth with whom He could share His heart and the secrets of the universe. Knowing the beginning from the end was an act worthy of pursuit, knowing there would one day be a people who would not turn their backs on Him or push Him away. After being delivered from Egypt through incredible signs and wonders, the children of Israel had been offered an invitation as a nation to come up on the mountain and see the Glory of God as Moses did. God wanted all of His children to know Him and shine with His Glory as Moses did; but instead, after being prepared three days, they turned down the invitation of the Lord because they were afraid of His presence (see Exod. 19:1-20).

The invitation was for all of Israel to come on the mountain into the Glory of God, seeing His Glory and being transformed in His presence, but fear caused them to shy away. They refused God for fear of dying on the mountain (see Exod. 20:18-21).

The Lord wanted all of His people to shine with His Glory.

The Lord wanted all of His people to shine with His Glory like Moses. They had seen the power of His signs and wonders and how God had crushed the strongest nation on the planet, delivering them from bondage with raw supernatural authority never witnessed before. Seeing all these things, they still refused His invitation to come up into the mountain of His presence. They were just too afraid of the power of His majesty.

Not too much further down the road, Moses had sent out ten spies to search out the land God had sworn to give the Israelites as an inheritance for them. The spies were gone 40 days scouting the land. When they returned they gave a report (see Num. 13:30-33).

The people were afraid to enter the land for fear of the giants. They talked about choosing for themselves a new captain and returning to the land of Egypt. But Moses and Aaron fell on their faces before all the assembly of the Israelites. Joshua and Caleb tried to quiet the people and talk sense to them (see Num. 14:8-9).

The congregation wouldn't hear what Joshua and Caleb had to say. They had made up their minds. They were going to kill Joshua and Caleb with stones and make a plan to return to the land of Egypt.

But right in the middle of their meeting, God showed up at the Tent of Meeting (see Num. 14:10-19). The Lord was so upset with the children of Israel that He told Moses He was going to destroy them all with pestilence and disinherit them and make from Moses a nation greater and mightier than they. But Moses pleaded Israel's case to God, and God listened to Moses. But hear the thing God said:

> *And the Lord said, "I have pardoned according to your word. But truly as I live and as all the earth shall be filled with the glory of the Lord"* (Numbers 14:20-21 AMP).

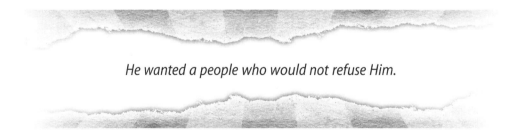

He wanted a people who would not refuse Him.

God swore by His own name that the earth would be filled with His Glory. He would have a people who would not refuse Him, a family in the earth who knows His ways and His paths—a supernatural people who know His Glory. This was the reason the Lord was angry with Israel. He revealed Himself over and over again to a stiff-necked people who chose not to believe in Him.

In the history of humankind, there has never been a generation of people to be filled with the Glory of the Lord, and I believe we are this generation. We are the Glory generation! I believe we are the people God was looking for, who will reveal the knowledge of the Glory of the Lord in the earth (see Hab. 2:14).

There is a rising Glory generation already shining with the radiance and splendor of His light. This body will not just have faith *in* God but will have the faith *of* God. They will look and act like God in the earth. They will understand that they too are filled with the fullness of the godhead—Father, Son, and Holy Spirit—and the Spirit of Holiness and resurrection power lives in them. They will become the gateway of God in the earth allowing Heaven to open up on them as Kingdom representatives. With this authority, they are able to act on God's behalf, destroying the works of the devil and establishing the will of Jesus everywhere they go. They will be filled with revelation knowledge, knowing how to implement righteousness and justice on the earth as God's magistrates and judiciaries. This is the rising Glory generation God was looking for. This is His Body on the earth.

Yes, it's true—Jesus Christ is coming back in the clouds one day, at the last-day trump; but before that day, He is coming back in and through a corporate Body of Christ in the earth. Jesus paid the ultimate price to restore us to right relationship with Himself, and now He is reaping the fruit of tears sown in the Garden of Gethsemane, for they who sow in tears will doubtless come again rejoicing, bringing in the sheaves. Jesus Christ paid a high price in blood to restore us to this place. The fruit is ripe in the earth and ready for harvest. Now is the time. Jesus has opened up the way back to Eden; He is the Tree of Life.

Questions to Ponder

What are some characteristics and qualities of this present rising Glory generation? What will their relationships with God look like? How will they represent God's Kingdom of power and Glory in the earth?

_____

_____

_____

_____

_____

Endnote

1.   Translated by R.H. Charles, *The Book of Enoch, Book 1: The Watchers,* http://www
.ancienttexts.org/library/ethiopian/enoch/index.html (accessed March 26, 2009), Chapters
13-15.

QUESTIONS FOR GROUP DISCUSSION

If you had been with the Israelites when God invited them up on the mountain to meet with Him (Exod. 20:18-21), would you have reacted in the same way they did? Why or why not? Read Hebrews 12:18-24 and look at the mountain God is inviting us to now! What are some differences between these two mountains (Sinai and Zion)?

_____

_____

_____

_____

_____

_____

_____

_____

_____

Read Second Corinthians 3-4. What are some contrasts between the Old and New Covenant? Why is the New Covenant superior? Where is the Light of the knowledge of the Glory of the Lord revealed?

_____

_____

_____

_____

_____

_____

_____

LIFE APPLICATION

Jeff Jansen gives us a picture of what we are to become: "the gateway of God in the earth allowing Heaven to open up on them as Kingdom representatives." What do you need to do to put yourself in a receiving position to become such a Kingdom representative?

_____

_____

_____

_____

_____

_____

_____

_____

_____

_____

_____

_____

_____

_____

_____

_____

_____

_____

GLORY RISING

BREAKTHROUGH PRAYER

Holy Spirit, I invite You to come into my life and fill my entire being with Your presence. I ask that You would apply the shed blood of Jesus Christ over my life—baptize me into His death and sanctify me from all ungodliness. If there is anyone I need to forgive, show me. If there is anything I must confess and ask forgiveness for, show me. It's my desire to follow You my whole life long. I don't want to hold anything back from You—take all of me! I surrender myself to You—I acknowledge that You are God and Lord of my life. Flood every area of my heart with Your life and light—let there be no untouched corner—no dark place in me.

Fill me, Holy Spirit, with Your presence, power, and anointing—raise me to new life in Christ Jesus. Impart to me a supernatural hunger to know you intimately—to fellowship and commune with You daily. Father God, thank You for making known Your Glory in my life.

I ask You right now for the Spirits of understanding and revelation to come rest upon me. I ask You to awaken my spirit to the spiritual truths presented in these writings, and that my mind would come into complete and total alignment with what the Spirit of God is speaking. I bind every spirit of confusion and every spirit of distraction in my life in Jesus' name—I command you to leave now. I ask for clarity of mind—I choose to focus my thoughts and set my heart on things above where I am seated with Christ in heavenly places. I ask that You would invade my life with Your presence, power, and Glory—saturate me with the electric presence of Heaven.

Teach me how to be a Kingdom ambassador in the earth today—a delegated, hand-picked representative of Jesus Christ. I wholly and entirely offer myself to You now as a living sacrifice—to Your name be the Kingdom, the power, and the Glory in all generations. In Jesus' name, Amen.

NOTES

NOTES

NOTES

Resources available from

GLOBAL FIRE MINISTRIES

CDs and CD Sets

The Visitation

Spiritual Secrets of Smith Wigglesworth

Destiny Doors

Heavenly Encounters and Angelic Visitations

Music

Believe

Spontaneous

The Eye of God (Instrumental)

The Eye of God—Wonders

Mystic Glory

Soaking Video (SV) Series

Acceleration into the Glory of God

More titles available through:

GLOBAL FIRE MINISTRIES
PMB 11
425 North Thompson Lane
Murfreesboro, TN 37129

E-mail: info@globalfireministries.com

Web site: www.globalfireministries.com

Phone Number: 615-867-1124

Additional copies of this book and other book titles from DESTINY IMAGE are available at your local bookstore.

Call toll-free: 1-800-722-6774.

Send a request for a catalog to:

Destiny Image® Publishers, Inc.

P.O. Box 310
Shippensburg, PA 17257-0310

"Speaking to the Purposes of God for This Generation and for the Generations to Come."

For a complete list of our titles, visit us at www.destinyimage.com.